The Saltwater Wetland

Life in the Sea

The Saltwater Wetland

Pam Walker and
Elaine Wood

Facts On File, Inc.

The Saltwater Wetland

Facts On File, Inc.
132 West 31st Street
New York NY 10001

Library of Congress Cataloging-in-Publication Data
Walker, Pam, 1958–
The saltwater wetland / Pam Walker and Elaine Wood.
p. cm.—(Life in the sea)
Includes bibliographical references and index.
ISBN 0-8160-5702-8 (hardcover)
1. Wetland ecology—Juvenile literature. 2. Wetlands—Juvenile literature.
I. Wood, Elaine, 1950– II. Title.
QH541.5.M3W326 2005
578.769—dc22   2004024224

Facts On File books are available at special discounts when purchased in bulk quantities for businesses, associations, institutions, or sales promotions. Please call our Special Sales Department in New York at
(212) 967-8800 or (800) 322-8755.

You can find Facts On File on the World Wide Web at
http://www.factsonfile.com

Text and cover design by Dorothy M. Preston
Illustrations by Dale Williams, Sholto Ainslie, and Dale Dyer

Printed in the United States of America

VB FOF 10 9 8 7 6 5 4 3 2 1

This book is printed on acid-free paper.

Contents

Preface

*L*ife first appeared on Earth in the oceans, about 3.5 billion years ago. Today these immense bodies of water still hold the greatest diversity of living things on the planet. The sheer size and wealth of the oceans are startling. They cover two-thirds of the Earth's surface and make up the largest habitat in this solar system. This immense underwater world is a fascinating realm that captures the imaginations of people everywhere.

Even though the sea is a powerful and immense system, people love it. Nationwide, more than half of the population lives near one of the coasts, and the popularity of the seashore as a home or place of recreation continues to grow. Increasing interest in the sea environment and the singular organisms it conceals is swelling the ranks of marine aquarium hobbyists, scuba divers, and deep-sea fishermen. In schools and universities across the United States, marine science is working its way into the science curriculum as one of the foundation sciences.

The purpose of this book is to foster the natural fascination that people feel for the ocean and its living things. As a part of the set entitled Life in the Sea, this book aims to give readers a glimpse of some of the wonders of life that are hidden beneath the waves and to raise awareness of the relationships that people around the world have with the ocean.

This book also presents an opportunity to consider the ways that humans affect the oceans. At no time in the past have world citizens been so poised to impact the future of the planet. Once considered an endless and resilient resource, the ocean is now being recognized as a fragile system in danger of overuse and neglect. As knowledge and understanding about the ocean's importance grow, citizens all over the world can participate in positively changing the ways that life on land interacts with life in the sea.

Acknowledgments

$\mathcal{T}$his opportunity to study and research ocean life has reminded both of us of our past love affairs with the sea. Like many families, ours took annual summer jaunts to the beach, where we got our earliest gulps of salt water and fingered our first sand dollars. As sea-loving children, both of us grew into young women who aspired to be marine biologists, dreaming of exciting careers spent nursing wounded seals, surveying the dark abyss, or discovering previously unknown species. After years of teaching school, these dreams gave way to the reality that we did not get to spend as much time in the oceans as we had hoped. But time and distance never diminished our love and respect for it.

We are thrilled to have the chance to use our own experiences and appreciation of the sea as platforms from which to develop these books on ocean life. Our thanks go to Frank K. Darmstadt, executive editor at Facts On File, for this enjoyable opportunity. He has guided us through the process with patience, which we greatly appreciate. Frank's skills are responsible for the book's tone and focus. Our appreciation also goes to Katy Barnhart for her copyediting expertise.

Special notes of appreciation go to several individuals whose expertise made this book possible. Audrey McGhee proofread and corrected pages at all times of the day or night. Diane Kit Moser, Ray Spangenburg, and Bobbi McCutcheon, successful and seasoned authors, mentored us on techniques for finding appropriate photographs. We appreciate the help of these generous and talented people.

Introduction

$\mathcal{S}$ ituated in coves and bays that physically protect them from the full force of the ocean, saltwater wetlands are unique coastal environments that form in the places where rivers and sea meet. Every saltwater wetland ecosystem, whether it be an estuary, mud flat, marsh, or mangrove forest has a unique character. Although thousands of saltwater wetlands exist on the seacoast worldwide, no two are exactly alike. Estuaries make up a large portion of these marine ecosystems.

If estuaries as a group have one constant quality, it is change. Each day brings the potential for fluctuations in temperature, water chemistry, and levels of nutrients. Consequently, very few kinds of organisms can make estuaries their permanent homes. The ones that are able to cope with these conditions find estuaries to be well-stocked storehouses and safe havens.

Because they offer young animals plenty of hiding places and good things to eat, estuaries provide nurseries for many fish and shellfish. In their warm, shallow waters, juveniles of hundreds of different species dart among submerged plants or move up and down the intertidal zone with the rhythm of the tides. After a few months of growth, they are better equipped to face their predators in the open ocean.

The Saltwater Wetland is one of a set of six books titled Life in the Sea. In these texts, we examine the physical features and biology of five distinct regions of the ocean: the beach and tidal zone, estuaries and saltwater wetlands, the coral reef, shallow water and the continental shelf, and the deep ocean. The sixth book explores the past and current impact humans have on oceans.

Chapter 1 of *The Saltwater Wetland* takes a look at the geology of estuarine systems, beginning at the end of the most recent Ice Age 18,000 years ago. At that time, the Earth's surface was transformed when millions of square miles of continental ice began to melt and flow to the oceans. The resulting water-filled coastal embayments took on the characteristics of both their terrestrial and aquatic systems borders. The estuaries formed by this ancient flood are still here today. Although each is unique in its own right, all estuaries share common chemical and physical characteristics. Many of an estuary's unique traits are due to the way water circulates in that system and the types of sediments that cover the estuary floor.

The critical roles played by microorganisms, fungi, and plants in saltwater wetlands are discussed in chapter 2. These organisms form the base of food chains that support other wetland residents. Photosynthesizing single-celled organisms, algae, and vascular plants all provide food for the animals that live in the system. The food webs of estuaries are atypical when compared to more familiar terrestrial systems. On the land, grazing animals eat most of the plant matter, and other animals in turn prey on them. However, in the estuary, very few animals eat the abundant cord grass, mangrove, and large algae. When these plants die, they fall to the estuary floor, where they are decomposed by fungi and heterotrophic bacteria. Instead of consuming plant matter, small animals in the estuary feed on these decomposers.

Chapters 3 and 4 take a close look at some of the many forms of invertebrate life in the estuary. Invertebrates, animals without backbones, are generally small organisms and include worms, clams, starfish, and shrimp. Sponges, animals that lack tissues and organs, are the simplest invertebrates. Cnidarians, a group that includes jellyfish and anemones, are more complex animals whose members are armed with stinging cells for defense and hunting. Comb jellies, a group of similar animals that lack stinging cells, are small organisms that float in the water column where they snare tiny bits of food. Worms are bottom dwellers that spend a lot of their time hiding from predators.

Most estuary visitors are familiar with common invertebrates like mollusks and crustaceans. Mollusks are a large group of animals that includes snails, clams, oysters, and octopuses, and crustaceans include shrimp and lobster. Horseshoe crabs, relatives of the crustaceans, are some of the most primitive animals in this group, and they have close ties to spiders. Echinoderms, animals that have spiny skin, are also abundant and include starfish and sea cucumbers.

Estuaries may be best known for their fish, the topic of chapter 5. Both commercial and recreational fishermen are familiar with the variety and abundance of fish that spend time in an estuary. Many species spawn near the estuary so their offspring can live within its borders while they mature and reach a size that might allow them to survive ocean predation. Others live their entire lives in the estuary, feasting year round. Some typical estuary fish include skates and rays, sharks, bass, eels, seatrout, and drums.

Chapter 6 looks at some of the other kinds of vertebrates that can be found in an estuary. A variety of reptiles, birds, and mammals all make their homes there. The saltwater crocodile is a resident of some Asian estuaries, where it serves as top predator in those food chains. Worldwide, a variety of sea turtles visit estuaries from time to time. Most are extremely large animals that resemble their smaller terrestrial relatives. However, sea turtles have adaptations like flippers to help them succeed in their marine environments. The number and kind of birds associated with estuarine systems is staggering. Both long- and short-legged waders, divers, and swimmers congregate there to feed on the small invertebrates or rich plant life. Mammals found in the estuary include harbor seals and a few species of whales and dolphins.

In chapter 7, we reflect on the current and future conditions of estuaries. Literally caught in the middle of frequent human activity and attention, estuaries are suffering from pollution, overdevelopment, and reductions in freshwater. With this in mind, we explore the need for sustainable growth.

Physical Characteristics
Chemistry and Geology of the Saltwater Wetland

*L*ife on Earth is sustained by one of the simplest compounds, water. Living things share the planet's supply of water, which is continuously distributed through an endless path known as the water cycle. By evaporating from waterways, soil, and living things, water travels to the atmosphere, where it condenses into liquid form and falls back to Earth.

Once returned to the surface as precipitation, water may take one of several paths. Water may sink into the soil to become part of an underground reservoir, or it might evaporate and return to the atmosphere to rejoin the clouds. The liquid can also be taken in by plants, animals, and other living things. A large portion of the water that falls back to Earth flows into streams and creeks. These small waterways join to form rivers, which eventually wind their way to the ocean.

In many cases, rivers flow into the sea within the boundaries of bays, areas that are partially closed off from the ocean. In these semi-enclosed regions, river freshwater and ocean salt water blend, forming bodies of water called estuaries. Estuarine water varies from fresh to salty, with much of it an intermediate mixture that is described as brackish. Along the coasts of the United States, more than 5,850 square miles (15,150 km²) of gulfs, inlets, bays, and sounds are classified as estuaries.

Tides have a strong influence on estuaries. Tidal impact on estuaries is so important that the term *estuary* is derived from the Latin word *aestuarium,* which translates as "tidal." Because its waters rise and fall with the regular movement of the tides, many of an estuary's unique characteristics are due to this tidal flux.

Estuaries are critically important to the health of coastal environments worldwide. They serve as homes to more kinds of living things than either the rivers that fill them or the oceans into which they flow. As a consequence, the *biodiversity* in estuarine systems is higher than in either of their parent systems. A high degree of biodiversity helps to ensure that a natural system is strong and healthy.

Estuaries are exceptionally productive places, and their abundance is due to several factors. All estuaries receive rich supplies of nutrients, experience good water circulation, and contain relatively warm waters. Nutrients in estuaries are derived from both the land and the ocean. The river donates dissolved minerals as well as organic matter that it collects as it travels over the land. Ocean water is also rich in minerals, including the salts that give it the distinctive salty flavor.

Good circulation guarantees that estuarine waters are well mixed. Mixing occurs in several ways. Rising and falling tides pick up and circulate minerals and organic matter, making them available to organisms in all parts of the system. Tides also stir the nitrogen and phosphorus-rich wastes that are generated by estuarine animals and microbes. Winds provide some mixing of nutrients in the uppermost layers. In addition, water flowing through the estuary rubs against the sides and bottom of the basin, creating turbulence that stirs the lower water column. This water movement at the bottom of the estuary keeps nutrients in suspension and prevents them from settling on the floor.

The productivity of estuaries and most other ecosystems depends on the work of plants. Plants require light to carry out the food-making process of photosynthesis. Although suspended sediments in the estuarine water may make it murky, much of the water is shallow enough for light to penetrate. In addition, receding tides expose mud flats—the homes of many one-celled green microorganisms—to the Sun.

The same factors that make estuaries productive also make them good homes to young fish and shellfish. Estuaries supply the immature animals with plenty of food as well as protection in the form of plant cover from predators. The young of most commercially important fish develop in these safe, well-stocked environments.

Salt marshes are found on the riverside of many low-lying estuaries. Depending on latitude, salt marshes may support lush growths of grasses, mangroves, or other plants that can tolerate brackish water. As the leaves, blades, stems and roots of plants fall to the estuary floor, they provide food for bacteria and fungi, which in turn serve as meals for larger organisms. In this way, rotting plant matter and living plant material form the basis for large food webs and complex communities.

Saltwater marshes represent the end stages of estuary life. Marshes are the areas of the estuary that are filling in with soil, slowly making the transition from marine to terrestrial environments. Marsh plants are responsible for most of this transformation. Their roots hold sediment in place, preventing it from washing back to sea when the tide recedes.

Normal changes in marshes and estuaries drive their evolution into terrestrial ecosystems. A young salt marsh is primarily made up of grasses. As tides bring in nutrients, grasses flourish and form thick, luxuriant meadows. Water flowing through the grasses is forced to slow down, and the material suspended in it settles out. Over time, so much sediment accumulates that the marsh floor finally builds up enough to escape the influence of the tides. As large sections of the marsh rise above tide levels, more landlike plants move in, quickly establishing a young terrestrial type of environment. Over time, the entire estuary fills in with soil and extends the adjacent landmass.

Salt marshes often border tidal flats, gently sloping stretches of unvegetated soil. With every change of tides, tidal flats are alternately covered by water or exposed to the air. They reach their greatest size during the spring tides, then shrink to much smaller scales two weeks later during neap tides. The areas of tidal flats that experience the least daily changes are those on the outermost edge. On the waterside, the base of the tidal flat most often remains submerged. On the land side, the tidal flat merges with the mature part of the saltwater marsh and is usually dry. The degree to which water covers the areas between these two extremes creates several zones, each of which has unique physical and chemical characteristics. Living things take up residence in the zones for which their particular adaptations are most suited.

Sediments in tidal flats are small-grained and unconsolidated, forming soft, muddy conditions. Most of the sediment material that covers a flat was moved there from the bottom of the estuary by incoming tides. With each receding tide, sedimentary structures like ripples, cracks, and rills form in the mud deposits. Ripples are patterns of waves that form on top of the sediment due to currents in the ebbing waters. Mud cracks appear when conditions are hot and dry and the sediment is baked. The tiny channels that form across the flats are called rills; water drains into them on its way back to the estuary.

Tidal flats are commonly found in the estuaries of low, broad tide plains. In the Bay of Fundy and the North Sea of Germany, tidal flats are extensive because water travels a long distance between high and low marks. On the other hand, tidal flat environments are absent in fjord-type estuaries, which have steep sides.

Origins of Estuaries

From a geologic point of view, estuaries are very young features on the Earth. Most of the present-day estuaries formed after the last Ice Age. There are more estuaries on the Earth now than there were in the past.

During the Ice Age, much of the water in the world's oceans was ice. The formation of ice effectively removed water from the oceans, causing sea levels to drop. As water levels went down, coastlines grew, extending past their old locations.

About 18,000 years ago, temperatures began to rise, and the Ice Age eventually came to an end. Warmer temperatures caused the continental glaciers covering much of Europe, Asia, and North America, as well as large sections of polar ice caps, to melt. Ocean water that had been trapped as ice returned to the ocean basin, and sea elevation rose. Rising water during this period created four basic types of estuaries, which are shown in Figure 1.1. These four types are coastal plain estuaries, fjords, bar-built estuaries, and tectonic estuaries.

During the Ice Age, as now, rivers flowed to the sea, gouging deep valleys on their way. When the Ice Age ended and sea levels rose, seawater ran back into some of the valleys that were created by ancient rivers. As a result, thousands of river valleys were "drowned," and coastal estuaries formed.

Examples of this type of estuary include the Chesapeake River Bay, the Hudson River Bay, and the Ashe Island Estuary of Charleston, South Carolina, shown in the upper color insert on page C-1.

Fjords, valleys of seawater that are bordered by sharp cliffs, were created in a similar way. During the recent Ice Age, glaciers carved slender, steep-sided valleys in some locations. As the glaciers moved forward, they pushed moraine, loads of rubble and soil, ahead of them. When the glaciers melted, the valleys they had gouged filled with seawater. In locations where rubble acted as sills and partially blocked the entrances to the valleys, estuaries formed.

Estuaries also arose in places where ocean currents created sandbars, deposits of sand and silt, a short distance from the shores. In an area where a sand bar partially closed off an inlet or bay fed by a river, a shallow estuary developed. The Charlotte Harbor is an example of a bar-built estuary.

Tectonic estuaries formed at the boundaries of active plates of the Earth's crust. The Earth's outermost layer, the crust, is not one solid skin. Instead, it is more like a mosaic made up of tiles or plates. The plates are constantly moving and shifting because of tectonic forces within the Earth. When tectonic plates shift, they generally change features on the Earth's surface. In the past, movements of the crust along the coast created depressions

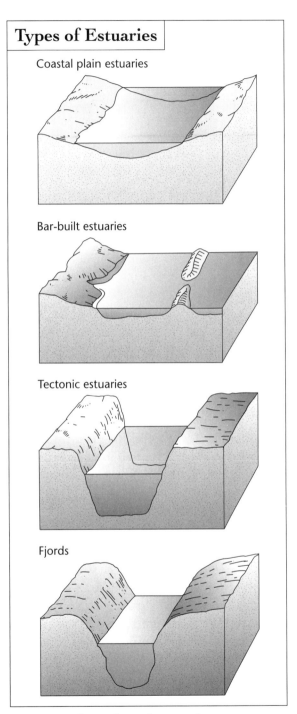

Fig. 1.1 *The geological types of estuaries are coastal plain, bar-built, and tectonic estuaries and fjords.*

into which rivers flowed. San Francisco Bay formed in this manner.

Features of the Estuary

Estuaries undergo changes on both a daily and seasonal basis. Some of these changes involve the volume of water in the estuary. Others have to do with the physical and chemical factors of the water, including salinity, temperature, levels of dissolved oxygen, and availability of nutrients.

In estuary systems, *salinity*, the amount of dissolved minerals or salts in water, is a critical chemical factor. Estuarine waters experience more variations in salinity than any other type of marine environment. Salinity can vary in a system from one day to the next and from one part of the estuary to another. Tides bring salt water in once or twice a day, depend-

Chemical and Physical Characteristics of Water

Water is one of the most widespread materials on this planet. Water fills the oceans, sculpts the land, and is a primary component in all living things. For all of its commonness, water is a very unusual molecule whose unique qualities are due to its physical structure.

Water is a compound made up of three atoms: two hydrogen atoms and one oxygen atom. The way these three atoms bond causes one end of the resulting molecule to have a slightly negative charge, and the other end a slightly positive charge. For this reason water is described as a polar molecule.

The positive end of one water molecule is attracted to the negative end of another water molecule. When two oppositely charged ends of water molecules get close enough to each other, a bond forms between them. This kind of bond is a hydrogen bond. Every water molecule can form hydrogen bonds with other water molecules. Even though hydrogen bonds are weaker than the bonds that hold together the atoms within a water molecule, they are strong enough to affect the nature of water and give this unusual liquid some unique characteristics.

Water is the only substance on Earth that exists in all three states of matter: solid, liquid, and gas. Because hydrogen bonds are relatively strong, a lot of energy is needed to separate water molecules from one another. That is why water can absorb more heat than any other material before

ing on the geographic location. The average salinity of ocean water is 35 parts per thousand, a measurement that is abbreviated as 35‰ (per mill). The symbol "‰" is similar to percent, but it refers to parts per thousand instead of parts per hundred. Freshwater, with salinity only slightly greater than 0‰, constantly flows into the system on one side.

Estuarine water is generally high in oxygen, but levels can vary with location and temperature. Because oxygen is required for the metabolism of countless organisms, its levels are critical. Oxygen enters water from two sources: air and plants. When water and air are actively mixed, oxygen dissolves in the water. In addition, marine plants give off oxygen during their food-making processes.

Several factors affect the amount of oxygen in estuary water. As water temperature increases, its ability to hold dissolved oxygen decreases. As a result, water is less oxygenated

its temperature increases and before it changes from one state to another.

Since water molecules stick to one another, liquid water has a lot of surface tension. Surface tension is a measure of how easy or difficult it is to break the surface of a liquid. These hydrogen bonds give water's surface a weak, membrane-like quality that affects the way water forms waves and currents. The surface tension of water also impacts the organisms that live in the water column, water below the surface, as well as those on its surface.

Atmospheric gases, such as oxygen and carbon dioxide, are capable of dissolving in water, but not all gases dissolve with the same ease. Carbon dioxide dissolves more easily than oxygen, and there is always plenty of carbon dioxide in seawater. On the other hand, water holds only $\frac{1}{100}$ the volume of oxygen found in the atmosphere. Low oxygen levels in water can limit the number and types of organisms that live there. The concentration of dissolved gases is affected by temperature. Gases dissolve more easily in cold water than in warm, so cold water is richer in oxygen and carbon dioxide than warm water. Gases are also more likely to dissolve in shallow water than deep. In shallow water, oxygen gas from the atmosphere is mixed with water by winds and waves. In addition, plants, which produce oxygen gas in the process of photosynthesis, are found in shallow water.

on hot days than on cool ones. As the salinity of water increases, its ability to hold dissolved oxygen decreases. Water on the ocean side of the estuary holds less oxygen than water on the river side.

Experiments have shown that in the surface water of a well-mixed estuary, dissolved oxygen (DO) may be as high as 9 mg/L. At this level, organisms have plenty of oxygen for respiration. Several factors can cause rapid declines in DO, especially when temperatures are high. For example, fast-growing algae can create dense colonies that use all of the available oxygen. In addition, the ever-expanding algal mass shades some of the cells from the sun. As algal cells die, they sink to the bottom of the estuary in clumps where bacteria feed on them. With plenty of food available, bacterial populations increase rapidly. Excessive bacterial activity uses oxygen beneath the surface and can quickly eliminate the available oxygen in the entire water column. If oxygen levels drop below 4 mg/L, fish begin to die.

Water Mixing in Estuaries

Estuaries are dynamic water systems where there is always a lot of physical, chemical, and biological activity. Two factors that are constantly changing, and therefore always influencing, estuarine conditions are the inflow of fresh water from the river and salt water from the ocean. These two sources of water affect the overall salinity of the estuary, and salinity is one of the factors that influences which organisms can live there.

River water is described as "fresh" because its salinity is extremely low, almost 0‰. Therefore, salinity is naturally very low at the mouth of the river, the area where river water enters the estuary. On the other hand salinity is high at the oceanside. When salt water and freshwater meet somewhere between the river and the ocean, they do not simply diffuse together, mixing of their own accord. Without an energetic force to combine the two, they form separate layers, with denser salt water on the bottom and less dense freshwater on the top.

In estuaries that have an energetic tidal flow, mixing of the two types of water does occur. A strong tidal flow combines salt water and freshwater from the top to bottom of the water column. Estuaries with weak tidal flows have much less mixing.

Based on the degree of mixing they experience, estuaries are classified into four primary types: salt wedge, well-mixed, partially mixed, and reverse (see Figure 1.2).

The simplest type, the salt wedge estuary, forms when large volumes of fresh riverine water flow into an inlet that has a low tidal range. River water, which is less dense than seawater, tends to form a layer in the upper water column. As the river flows from its source, it is met by denser salt water from the ocean flowing into the inlet. The heavier salt water forms a wedge or tongue under the freshwater. The position of this wedge in the estuary varies constantly, moving closer to the mouth of the river at high tide and further from the mouth at low tide. In addition, seasons affect the wedge's location. During seasons when precipitation and river discharge are low, the wedge is closer to the river's mouth than in

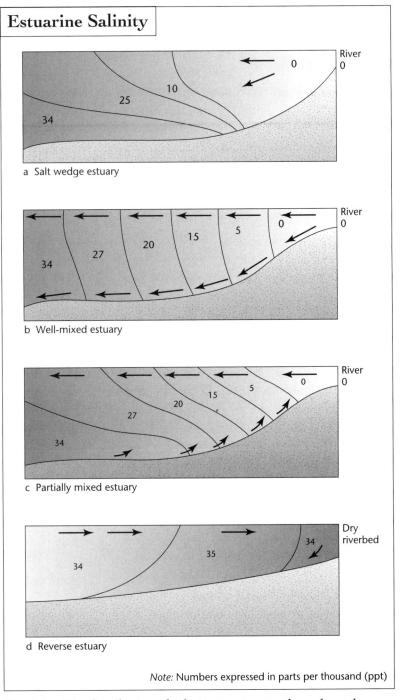

Estuarine Salinity

a Salt wedge estuary

b Well-mixed estuary

c Partially mixed estuary

d Reverse estuary

Note: Numbers expressed in parts per thousand (ppt)

Fig. 1.2   *The distribution of salinity in estuaries depends on the balance of salt water and freshwater entering and leaving the systems. Salinity is expressed in parts per thousand (1/1000).*

Tides

Tides result from a combination of three forces: the gravitational force of the Sun, the gravitational force of the Moon, and the motion of the Earth. Gravity is the force of attraction, or pull, between two bodies. Everything that has mass exerts gravity. The Earth and Moon exert gravitational pulls on each other. Because the Earth has more mass than the Moon, its gravity keeps the Moon in orbit. The Moon does not fall into the Earth because of the inertia, the tendency of a moving object to keep moving, that is created by their stable orbits.

The inward force of gravity and the outward force of inertia affect the entire surface of the Earth, but not to the same degree. Owing to Earth's rounded shape, the equator is closer to the Moon than Earth's poles are. The pull of the Moon's gravity is consequently stronger around the equator. On the side of the Earth facing the Moon at any given time, the Moon's gravity pulls the Earth toward it. The solid Earth is unable to respond dramatically to that pull, but the liquid part of Earth can. As a result, the ocean bulges out toward the Moon on the side of Earth that is facing it. On the side that is farthest from the Moon, inertia flings water away from the Moon. The Moon's pull on one side of Earth and the force of inertia on the opposite side create two bulges—high tides—in the ocean.

The bulges do not rotate around the Earth as it turns on its axis. Instead, they remain aligned with the Moon as the Earth rotates under them. Different parts of the Earth move into and out of these bulges as it goes through one rotation, or one day.

Even though the Sun is much farther from Earth than the Moon is, the Sun also has an effect on tides. The Sun's influence is only about half that of the Moon's. A small solar bulge on Earth follows the Sun throughout the day, and the side of the Earth opposite the Sun experiences a small inertial bulge.

The Moon revolves around the Earth in a 28-day cycle. As it does so, the positions of the Moon, Earth, and Sun relative to one another change. The three bodies are perfectly aligned during two phases: new moon and full moon, as shown in Figure 1.3. At these times, the Sun and Moon forces are acting on the same area of Earth at the same time, causing high tide to be at its highest and low tide to be at its lowest. These extremes are known as spring tides and occur every two weeks.

During first- and third-quarter conditions, when only one-half of the Moon is visible in the night sky, the Sun and Moon are at right angles to the Earth. In these positions, their gravitational pulls are working against each other, and the two bodies cancel each other's effects to some degree, causing high tides to be at their lowest, and low tides to be at their highest. These neap tides also occur every two weeks.

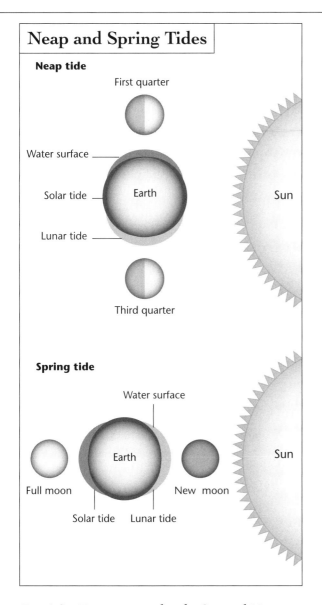

Neap and Spring Tides

Neap tide

First quarter

Water surface

Solar tide — Earth — Sun

Lunar tide

Third quarter

Spring tide

Water surface

Full moon — Earth — New moon — Sun

Solar tide   Lunar tide

Fig. 1.3   Every two weeks, the Sun and Moon are aligned with Earth so that the gravitational forces of both heavenly bodies create very high tides called spring tides. When the Moon and Sun are at right angles to Earth, lower, or neap, tides result.

seasons of rain, when the fresh-water keeps the wedge of salt water pushed back toward the ocean. Examples of salt wedge estuaries are those found at the mouths of the Columbia, Hudson, Amazon, Congo, and Mississippi Rivers.

If the tidal flow is very strong and the water relatively shallow, an entirely different scenario develops in the estuary. Strong tidal influx mixes the two waters together, resulting in a well-mixed estuary containing water of equal salinity from top to bottom. The entire system is constantly pushed toward the sea by the strength of the river flow. The Delaware River, the Columbia River, and the Bay of Fundy are well-mixed estuaries.

In bays that have relatively deep water and strong tidal flow, an estuary develops that is intermediate between the well-mixed and salt wedge types. This type is called a partially mixed estuary, and it shares properties of both extremes. The salt water and freshwater do not form a distinct wedge because some mixing occurs at their interface. San Francisco Bay, the Chesapeake Bay, and both the Thames and Mersey Rivers in England are examples of partially mixed estuaries.

The fourth type, the reverse estuary, is found along hot, dry coasts like those of the Baja Peninsula and in the gulfs of South Australia. During the driest periods of the year, freshwater stops flowing into the estuary. Since evaporating water does not carry dissolved salts along with it, continuous evaporation causes salts to accumulate in the upper layers. Water lost through evaporation is replaced by water from the ocean flowing in under it. The result is an upper layer that is saltier than water beneath it. Reverse estuaries are found on the Pacific coast of the Baja Peninsula, along the Gulf coast, and along some of the gulfs of South Australia.

Sediments

Sediments, solid pieces of matter that result from the weathering of rock and the breakdown of organic matter, are transported by water or wind. The material that makes up sediments may be organic, from living things, or inorganic, from nonliving material. Sediments carried in water often settle and accumulate on the bottom of the estuary, in the salt marsh, and on the tidal flats, giving those substrates their unique characteristics.

Sediments are denser than water, so they cannot remain suspended unless the water is moving. Moving water can lift and transport particles from one place to another. As water slows, the largest, heaviest particles settle first.

In rivers, the turbulence of moving water forms currents and eddies that help hold sediment particles in suspension. The more turbulent the water, the more sediment it can hold and the darker and murkier it appears. As a river enters an estuary, the water slows down and particles begin to drift to the estuary floor. On the other side of the estuary, tidal currents also carry a load of sediment. As they flow into the estuarine system, they also slow and deposit some of their load.

The points in the estuary where sediments are deposited depend on the relative strengths of the river and the tides. In salt wedge estuaries that have strong riverine flow, the dissolved minerals and suspended matter of the river are swept along on top of the denser saltwater from the ocean. If the river flow is strong enough, much of the dissolved and particulate matter is carried out of the estuary into the sea. In systems with less robust river flow, water begins to slow down and drop portions of its load near the point of entry, at the estuary head.

In mixed estuaries, suspended material that is carried in by river water gets combined evenly from the top to the bottom of the water column. When mixing occurs, it dramatically slows the motion and speed of the river water and gives the suspended matter time to settle. As a result, sediment can fall out of solution and accumulate in the upper part of the estuary. This creates an area of cloudy water that is known as the region of maximum turbidity.

Soil particles like those suspended in river water can be classified into three sizes: sand, silt, and clay. The pattern of their deposition across the estuary floor depends on the size of the particles as well as strength of the tides and river currents. Sand is the largest and coarsest of the three types, so it falls out of suspension first. Because sand particles have irregular shapes, they do not fit close together. Open spaces between particles allow oxygen to circulate freely. Sands deposited on the tidal flats drain well and do not retain water, so air pockets form between the grains and conditions are aerobic, or oxygen-rich.

Silt is made of soil particles that are smaller and smoother than sand. As a result, particles of silt can pack together more closely than those of sand. Silt also contains more organic matter than sand. Silt that is deposited on the tidal flat or salt marsh does not drain readily during low tide. When soil retains water, oxygen cannot circulate between the particles, and the material becomes anaerobic, or free of oxygen. Anaerobic soils support an entirely different group of organisms than aerobic soils. Many anaerobic microorganisms are responsible for the rotten-egg smell that is associated with the bottoms and edges of estuaries.

Clay is the smallest soil particle, and clay particles pack tightly together. As a result, they hold water very well and almost always form anaerobic environments. Much of the tidal flats of drowned river valleys are made up of the thick, sticky muds of clays.

Sediment may stay in an estuary permanently or it may travel on to the sea. The greater the river output, the faster sediment moves out of the estuarine system. When river discharge is low, sediment drifts to the estuary floor and simply travels back and forth with the tides, never leaving the system. In these low-energy estuaries, occasional flooding is the only way to flush the sediments out. In some regions floods are essential events for moving trapped sediments out of the estuaries and into the ocean or onto the soil. Without flushing, sediment builds up in the estuary and fills it quickly.

Because of the minerals, nutrients, and sediments they receive, estuaries are important sites of nutrient recycling. Nutrients deposited in the soil and suspended in the water are either taken up by plants or recycled by microorganisms. Plants absorb nutrients through their cells and use them for their own growth. When plants die, their body parts fall to the estuary floor where they are converted back into simple materials by bacteria and fungi, making the minerals in them available once again for use by living things.

Two of the most important minerals are nitrogen and phosphorous. Both are essential elements used by algae and plants to formulate the compounds that make up their cellular structures. Of the two, nitrogen is most often in short supply.

Atmospheric nitrogen is extremely abundant, but it is not in a form that most living things can use. Microorganisms release usable nitrogen by breaking down complex compounds in animal wastes and the tissues of dead organisms. Some of the nitrogen is taken up for their own purposes; the rest is freed into the environment. Plants take advantage of nitrogen provided in this decomposition process and use it to grow. Animals then get the nitrogen their bodies require by eating plants or by consuming animals that eat plants. The estuarine environment also supports a group of very simple microbes called cyanobacteria that are able to take up nitrogen directly from the air. Very few other types of organisms can perform this feat, and their presence enriches nitrogen levels in the system.

Conclusion

Estuaries and their bordering saltwater wetlands are dynamic environments that form in protected coastal areas where rivers meet the oceans. Although thousands of estuaries exist worldwide, no two are exactly alike structurally, physically, or chemically. Estuaries as a group represent some of the most productive areas on Earth. By some estimates they are as productive as coral reefs and tropical rain forests.

The high productivity of estuaries is a direct result of their physical and chemical characteristics. Estuarine waters are rich in nutrients from both the land and the ocean. The river input, wind energy, and tidal influx cause mixing that keeps nutrients distributed throughout the habitat and stirs oxygen into the water. In addition, estuaries are relatively shallow basins, and therefore warmer and more completely penetrated by light, than their neighboring, deeper saltwater environments.

Depending on the relative strengths of their saltwater and freshwater inputs, estuaries can be classified as salt wedge, well-mixed, partially mixed, and reverse, although many fall in between these clear definitions. A salt wedge system is dominated by a strong flow of freshwater from a river and tends to form strata of freshwater and salt water. A well-mixed estuary is subjected to stirring by strong tidal currents and therefore has about the same salinity throughout. If the water basin is deep, the estuary may be partially mixed, displaying characteristics of both the salt wedge and well-mixed types. In dry climates where evaporation rates are high, reverse estuaries are more saline in the upper layers than in the lower.

The type of sediment that is deposited in an estuary affects the kinds of organisms that can survive there. Particles of sediment may be made of sand, silt, or clay, depending on their origin. Sand, the largest, most irregularly shaped type of particle, tends to form sediments that support oxygen-dependent organisms. Clay, on the other hand, is a small particle that packs together so tightly that oxygen cannot penetrate it. Silt forms sediments that are intermediate between clay and sand.

Most estuarine sediments are a mixture of several types of particles, although in any system, one size may dominate.

The physical, chemical, and structural properties of estuaries define their characteristics and set the stage for the kinds of living things that can make their homes there. In most estuaries, conditions support lush growths of green plants, algae, and one-celled photosynthesizers. These organisms form the basis for the complex estuarine food webs.

2

Microbes and Plants
Producers and Decomposers
in the Saltwater Wetland

$\mathcal{T}$he estuary and its associated environments—the salt marshes and tidal flats—are dynamic ecosystems that support dense populations of organisms. The variety and numbers of microbes, fungi, and plants are enormous. Microorganisms and fungi are invisible to the casual observer. Despite their low profiles, these unseen creatures are essential in nutrient production and recycling. The more visible plants, both marine and semiterrestrial types, support large estuarine animal populations. Each organism contributes to the well-being of the ecosystem as a whole and plays essential roles in its food webs.

Fig. 2.1 Mangroves, with their extensive roots, are dominant plants in tropical estuarine systems. (Courtesy of NOAA Corps Collection)

Food Chains and Photosynthesis

Living things must have energy to survive. In an ecosystem, the path that energy takes as it moves from one organism to another is called a food chain. The Sun is the major source of energy for most food chains. Organisms that can capture the Sun's energy are called producers, or autotrophs, because they are able to produce food molecules. Living things that cannot capture energy must eat food and are referred to as consumers, or heterotrophs. Heterotrophs that eat plants are herbivores, and those that eat animals are carnivores. Organisms that eat plants and animals are described as omnivores.

When living things die, another group of organisms in the food chain—the decomposers, or detritivores—uses the energy tied up in the lifeless bodies. Detritivores break down dead or decaying matter, returning the nutrients to the environment. Nutrients in ecosystems are constantly recycled through interlocking food chains called food webs. Energy, on the other hand, cannot be recycled. It is eventually lost to the system in the form of heat.

Autotrophs can capture the Sun's energy because they contain the green pigment chlorophyll. During photosynthesis, detailed in Figure 2.2, autotrophs use the Sun's energy to rearrange the carbon atoms from carbon dioxide gas to form glucose molecules. Glucose is the primary food or energy source for living things. The hydrogen and oxygen atoms needed to form glucose come from molecules of water. Producers give off the extra oxygen atoms that are generated during photosynthesis as oxygen gas.

Autotrophs usually make more glucose than they need, so they store some for later use. Heterotrophs consume this stored glucose to support their own life processes. In the long run, it is an ecosystem's productivity that determines the types and numbers of organisms that can live there.

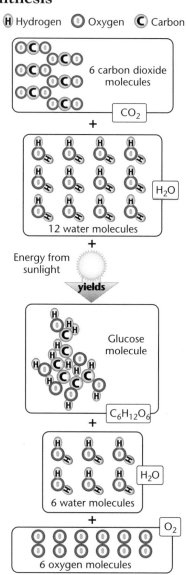

H Hydrogen O Oxygen C Carbon

6 carbon dioxide molecules CO_2

+

12 water molecules H_2O

+

Energy from sunlight   **yields**

Glucose molecule $C_6H_{12}O_6$

+

6 water molecules H_2O

+

6 oxygen molecules O_2

Fig. 2.2 *During photosynthesis, the energy of sunlight is used to rearrange the components of carbon dioxide and water molecules to form glucose, water, and oxygen.*

As a group, all of the green organisms make estuaries some of the most productive environments on Earth. Many estuarine plants are grasses that are close relatives of the grasses of terrestrial environments. Healthy populations of green microbes and multicelled algae also grow there. In temperate regions, the dominant salt marsh vegetation is cord grass, shown in the lower color insert on page C-1. Mangrove trees, like those in Figure 2.1, are the principle plants in tropical estuaries. Very few animals eat either of these plants directly. When the plants die, microbes and fungi break them down, converting the complex compounds that make up their tissues into simpler substances. Both dead plant material and its decomposers serve as food for other organisms.

On the tidal flats, the situation is different. The surfaces of tidal flats do not support large plants but instead are homes of green, one-celled organisms. Much of the photosynthesis on tidal flats is carried out by unicellular organisms called diatoms, as well as some species of filamentous algae. The productivity of plants and green microbes provides the food that supports the estuarine food chains.

Bacteria in the Estuary

The most numerous organisms on Earth are simple, one-celled microbes called bacteria. Many are heterotrophs that feed on dissolved organic matter in the water. Others are autotrophs that use the Sun's energy to make their own food. Both types are plentiful in the estuaries, salt marshes, and tidal flats.

Heterotrophic bacteria play critical roles in estuarine food webs. Along with fungi, they decompose, or break down, complex organic material into simple compounds. Without their work, the nutrients and minerals that living things need to survive would be tied up in the bodies of dead organisms and consequently lost to the ecosystem.

In most terrestrial food chains, like the ones found in forests or grasslands, plants capture the Sun's energy, herbivores graze on the plants, and carnivores feed on the herbivores. The major food chains in estuarine systems are different because they begin with the detritivores. In detritus-based food chains, very few herbivores eat the plants. When the plants die, their leaves, stems, and other parts drift to the substrate, where heterotrophic bacteria and fungi colonize them. These organisms feed on the plant parts and use them for their own energy. In addition, they break down the complex compounds in the plants and release them into the ecosystem. As small animals and other types of microorganisms feed on these bits of plant matter, they also consume the organisms that are attached to them. In this way, the energy of the plants moves from decomposers into the animal population.

Tidal flats and substrates of the marsh and estuary support large populations of heterotrophic bacteria. In the process of breaking down plant debris, these organisms can quickly consume all of the oxygen in the soil. Fresh oxygen does not

Kingdoms of Living Things

There are millions of different kinds of living things on Earth. To study them, scientists called taxonomists classify organisms by their characteristics. The first taxonomist was Carolus Linnaeus (1707–78), a Swedish naturalist who separated all creatures into two extremely large groups, or kingdoms: Plantae (plants) and Animalia (animals). By the middle of the 19th century, these two kingdoms had been joined by the newly designated Protista, the microscopic organisms, and Fungi. When microscopes advanced to the point that taxonomists could differentiate the characteristics of microorganisms, Protista was divided to include the kingdom Monera. By 1969, a five-kingdom classification system made up of Monera (bacteria), Protista (protozoans),

Fungi, Animalia, and Plantae was established. The five-kingdom system is still in use today, although most scientists prefer to separate monerans into two groups, the kingdom Archaebacteria and the kingdom Eubacteria.

Monerans are the smallest creatures on Earth, and their cells are much simpler than the cells of other living things. Monerans that cannot make their own food are known as bacteria and include organisms such as *Escherichia coli* and *Bacillus anthracis.* Photosynthetic monerans are collectively called cyanobacteria, and include *Anabaena affinis* and *Leptolyngbya fragilis.* In the six-kingdom classification system, the most common monerans, those that live in water, soil, and on other living things, are placed in the kingdom Eubacteria. Archae-

readily penetrate the tightly packed, waterlogged mud particles that cover much of the flats. As a result, sediments just beneath the surface are usually anoxic, or lacking oxygen. Once the oxygen is gone, anaerobic bacteria, which require oxygen-free environments, move in. Many of these are green sulfur bacteria, organisms that get the energy they need from sulfur compounds. As a by-product they create hydrogen sulfide, a gas that smells like rotten eggs and is often associated with salt marsh environments.

All of the autotrophic bacteria are collectively known as *cyanobacteria.* These cells contain chlorophyll as well as two other light-catching molecules: phycocyanin, a blue pigment, and phycoerthrin, a red one. The presence of these two accessory pigments helps the cells capture wavelengths of energy

bacteria are the inhabitants of extreme situations, such as hot underwater geothermal vents or extremely salty lakebeds.

Another kingdom of one-celled organisms, Protista, includes amoeba, euglena, and diatoms. Unlike monerans, protists are large, complex cells that are structurally like the cells of multicellular organisms. Members of the Protista kingdom are a diverse group varying in mobility, size, shape, and feeding strategies. A number are autotrophs, some heterotrophs, and others are mixotrophs, organisms that can make their own food and eat other organisms, depending on the conditions dictated by their environment.

The Fungi kingdom consists primarily of multicelled organisms, like molds and mildews, but there are a few one-celled members, such as the yeasts. Fungi cannot move around, and they are unable to make their own food because they do not contain chlorophyll. They are heterotrophs that feed by secreting digestive enzymes on organic material, then absorbing that material into their bodies.

The other two kingdoms, Plantae and Animalia, are also composed of multicelled organisms. Plants, including seaweeds, trees, and dandelions, do not move around but get their food by converting the Sun's energy into simple carbon compounds. Therefore, plants are autotrophs. Animals, on the other hand, cannot make their own food. These organisms are heterotrophs, and they include fish, whales, and humans, all of which must actively seek the food they eat.

that green chlorophyll cannot trap, making them very efficient photosynthesizers. The accessory pigments also account for the wide range of colors in cyanobacteria.

Free-living cyanobacteria are so minute that individuals are invisible in the water column or on top of the mud or sand. However, some species grow in colonies that look like green, red, or blue-green stains on the soil. *Lyngbya aestuarii* is a cyanobacteria that forms smooth mats on the tidal flats. At low tides, the masses of bacterial cells glisten on the flats, reflecting light from the gelatinous sheaths surrounding their cells. Mats of *Lyngbya* can be found where intertidal flats are regularly covered with water. Cells that make up the mats are so tightly packed that oxygen cannot diffuse through them. As a result, they create anoxic environments in the soil beneath them that are usually colonized by anaerobic heterotrophic bacteria.

Protists and Fungi

Although monerans and protists are both single-celled organisms, the cells of protists are much larger and more complex than those of bacteria. Protists make their homes in all parts of the estuary. To support their nutritional needs, the cells use a variety of feeding strategies and may be autotrophs, heterotrophs, or mixotrophs, green organisms that can make their own food or absorb nutrients.

Some of the key producers in estuarine systems are autotrophic protists called diatoms, shown in the upper color insert on page C-8. Diatoms that live on the surfaces of tidal flat sediments produce as much energy for the estuarine system as the large algae or the advanced plants that live there. Diatoms, sometimes called the "golden algae," are one-celled organisms that contain chlorophyll plus a brown-gold, light-absorbing pigment. There are hundreds of types of diatoms, but they share many common characteristics. Most build protective boxes around themselves called frustules.

The frustules of diatoms are primarily composed of silicon, a mineral found in sand and glass. Each microscopic box is a delicate, transparent cage that protects the unicellular organism within but lets in light so the cell can carry out photosynthesis. Frustules are perforated with hundreds of tiny openings that enable the cells to interact with their environment. Although the shapes of diatoms vary from elongated to round, most species that live on the tidal flats are the elongated type. Details of frustules, like the patterns created by the perforations, vary by species.

Like most protists, diatoms reproduce by *binary fission,* an *asexual* method in which the parent cell divides into two identical cells. Only one parent is required for asexual reproduction, and the two resulting offspring are clones, or exact duplicates, of the parent. During fission, diatoms also divide their frustules. When a parent diatom cell splits to forms two "daughter" cells, each daughter inherits one-half of the parent's frustule. The inherited halves become lids for each daughter cell, and both daughters grow new lower halves. As a result, one cell is the same size as the parent, and one is smaller. Over several generations, cells and frustules become too small to divide further. To solve the problem, the organisms leave their old, undersized frustules then either undergo a period of growth or go through sexual reproduction.

Sexual reproduction, which requires two parents, can occur in several ways. In some species, a small diatom cell breaks apart into little pieces, each of which swims around until it finds another diatom cell with which it can fuse. The cell that results from their fusion builds a new frustule. In other species, two adult diatom cells line up beside each other. Each cell undergoes division, then they exchange one daughter cell. The new pairs of daughter cells fuse, resulting in two new cells, each possessing genetic material from two parents. These two new cells construct new frustules.

Diatoms living on tidal flats are critically important producers, and they are well adapted for life in the constantly changing zone between land and water. When the tide comes in, they sink below the surface of the sediment to avoid being washed away. When the tide goes out, the cells migrate back up to the surface where they can take advantage of the sunlight. Diatoms lack some of the structures that other single-celled organisms have for locomotion. To move they secrete a layer of mucus, then glide over it. Because this mucus is very sticky, it glues particles of sediment together. As a result, the presence of diatoms helps stabilize sediments and slow erosion on tidal flats.

Life on the surface of the tidal flats exposes diatoms to drying, fluctuating temperatures and high doses of ultraviolet radiation from the Sun. Any type of cell exposed to these stressful conditions produces charged particles called free radicals. Free radicals are damaging to cells because they are capable of altering DNA, the genetic material in living things. To cope with this problem, diatoms generate unusually large volumes of enzymes that break down and destroy free radicals, thus protecting themselves from harm.

Along with heterotrophic bacteria, fungi are important detritivores in estuarine environments. These multicelled organisms decompose dead plant and animal matter that accumulates on the estuary floor, in the salt marsh, and on the sediments of the tidal flats. Fungi grow across the bodies of dead plants and animals by sending out tiny filaments called *hyphae*. Hyphae release enzymes that dissolve the plant and animal tissues, creating liquefied material that fungal cells can absorb.

The types of fungi that live in estuaries vary according to region, weather conditions, and other estuarine inhabitants. In the tropics, several marine fungi dwell among the mangrove trees. When mangrove leaves fall into the estuary water, fungi that can digest sugars quickly coat the leaves and begin breaking down their stores of glucose. Fungi that are capable of decomposing the tougher lignin compounds, which are components of the woody parts of mangroves, grow on dead roots, stems, and limbs. Most of the mangrove fungi are invisible to the naked eye, but a few, such as *Halocyphina villosa*, *Hypoxylon oceanicum*, *Verruculina enalia*, and several species of *Lutworthia*, can be seen with a hand lens.

Halocyphina villosa flourishes on the floor of the mangrove estuary where it forms round, white fruiting bodies, which are structures that release spores. Black fruiting bodies are produced on lower branches and twigs of mangrove trees by *Verruculina enalia*. This species is one of the dominant marine fungi on woody materials. Several species of *Lutworthia* flourish on mangrove leaves that fall on the substrate. Their black, filamentous fruiting bodies spread across blades of grasses as well as rotting leaves of mangrove trees.

Plants in the Estuary

Marine plants fall into two major categories: macroalgae and vascular plants. Macroalgae, or seaweeds, are multicellular structures with unique adaptations for their marine habitats. Seaweeds are classified according to their colors: green, red, and brown. Each macroalga's specific coloration depends on the combination of pigments it contains. Estuaries are home to species of algae of all three colors, as well as to several advanced plants.

In estuarine environments, macroalgae are not the chief food producers as they are in many marine locales. Instead, most of the production of food is carried out by cyanobacteria, diatoms, and vascular plants. The few species of macroalgae that grow in estuaries occur in patches where the substrate is firm and the water shallow enough to allow plenty of light penetration.

Some of the green macroalgae found in estuaries include *Blidingia minima, Cladophora rupestris, Ulva lactuca, Enteromorpha intestinalis, Derbesia marina,* as well as species of *Gelidium* and *Gracilaria. Blidingia minima* grows in the form of hollow tubes that reach heights of about 2 inches (5 cm). The tubes arise from round, flat *holdfasts* that are usually attached to rock. The taller, green macroalga *Cladophora rupestris* grows as dense, dark green or blue tufts. The stout *blades* are branched, and they grow in a circular pattern from the plant's base.

The paper-thin sheets of bright green *Ulva* are translucent because they are only two cell layers thick. Sheets may be free-floating or attached to the substrate with small, disc-shaped holdfasts. *Ulva*'s alternation of generations reproductive strategy is typical of many kinds of algae. One generation produces eggs and sperm, which unite to form a generation of organisms that manufacture and release spores. The plants

Light and Algal Coloration

Light is a form of energy that travels in waves. When the Sun's light arrives at Earth, it has a white quality to it. White light is made up of the colors red, orange, yellow, green, blue, indigo, and violet. The color of light is dependent on the length of the light wave. Light in the visible spectrum contains colors and has wavelengths between 0.4 and 0.8 microns (1 micron equals $\frac{1}{1,000,000}$ of a meter, or .000001 m; a micron is also known as a micrometer). Violet light has the shortest wavelength in the visible spectrum and red has the longest.

Light is affected differently by water than it is by air. Air transmits light, but water can transmit, absorb, and reflect light. Water's ability to transmit light makes it possible for photosynthesis to take place beneath the surface. All of the wavelengths of visible light are not transmitted equally, however; some penetrate to greater depths than others.

Light on the red side of the spectrum is quickly absorbed by water as heat, so red only penetrates to 49.2 feet (15 m). Blue light is not absorbed as much, so it penetrates the deepest, reaching 100 feet (33 m). Green light, in the middle of the spectrum, reaches intermediate depths. When light enters water that is filled with particles such as dirt and plant matter, as in an estuary, it takes on a greenish brown hue because it only penetrates far enough to strike, and be reflected from, the particles. In tropical water where particulate levels are very low, light travels much deeper before it reaches enough particles to be reflected back to the surface, so tropical water appears blue. Below 1,500 feet (457.2 m), no light is able to penetrate.

Because of the way light behaves in water, aquatic plants do not receive as much of the Sun's energy as do plants on land. To compensate, most species contain some accessory pigments, chemicals that are adept at capturing blue and green light. These accessory pigments provide the plants additional light and thereby help macroalgae increase their rate of photosynthesis. Some of these pigments mask the green of chlorophyll and give colors to macroalgae that are not usually associated with plants. Accessory pigments explain why seaweed occurs in shades of brown, gold, and red. Green algae contain accessory pigments, too, but they do not mask the color of chlorophyll as the pigments in other kinds of algae do.

that result from spores develop reproductive cells that undergo meiosis, a type of cell division that reduces the genetic material within the cell by one-half. This generation then produces egg and sperm once again.

Enteromorpha intestinalis has shimmering, bright green blades that are tubular in shape. The blades are filled with gas and irregularly constricted, giving them the appearance of intestines. Blades grow 12 inches (30 cm) long from small holdfasts that are secured to soil or rock. Gases contained in the algae's fronds help keep them afloat at the surface of the water. To ensure that offspring will be widely dispersed, *Enteromorpha intestinalis* releases its spores during a rising tide.

The estuary is home to many species of brown algae. Brown algae contain chlorophyll as well as accessory pigments that give them colors ranging from yellow to black. Most types of brown algae produce chemicals that protect the plants from predators. Several species are found in the estuary, including common kelp (*Laminaria saccharina*), saw wrack (*Fucus serratus*), flat wrack (*Fucus spirali*), and bladder wrack (*Fucus visiculosus*).

Brown, slippery fronds of *Fucus* plants grow to 20 inches (50 cm) in length. Each frond is equipped with air *bladders* that keep the plant afloat near the water's surface. The stipes and fronds synthesize a gel-like material, alginate, which gives the plant flexibility so it can move with the flow of water. Alginate also conserves moisture, protecting the plant when conditions are dry. Reproductive structures are wartlike knobs on the ends of the fronds that release gametes into seawater, where they unite to start new plants.

Tufted red weed (*Gigartina stellata*), Irish moss (*Chondrus crispus*), and laver (*Porphyra*) are red algae common in estuaries. Irish moss is a small, purplish-red seaweed that grows to 7.8 inches (20 cm). The wide, flat fronds of Irish moss look iridescent underwater but take on a green color in strong light. In Ireland, the plant was once collected by hand and used to make a milk-based pudding. Today, the alga is commercially harvested and processed for the gel-like carbohydrate in its cell walls, which is used as a thickener in many foods.

Lavers are seaweeds that look like purple, membranous sheets. Depending on the species, these plants vary from 4 to 20 inches (10 to 50 cm) in length. Like most red algae, the reproductive cycles of *Porphyra* are complex and include a two-year alternation of generations. An asexual *thallus* releases spores that develop into sexual plants. These produce egg and sperm that combine to form zygotes. The zygotes undergo cell division, forming spores that settle on the shells of animals like crabs. The spores grow into filamentous structures that bore into their hosts' shells. The shell-boring phase of *Porphyra* matures and produces spores that undergo meiosis. These daughter cells settle to the bottom and grow into new thalli, bringing the process back in a full circle.

Vascular Plants in the Estuary

Although macroalgae are important players in estuarine ecosystems, they are not the primary large plants there. Vascular plants such as sea grasses, mangroves, and cord grass produce the bulk of the food. These true plants first evolved to live on the land, then moved to the sea where they adapted to life in shallow salt water. Therefore they have many of the typical terrestrial plant adaptations like roots, vascular systems, pollen, and seeds.

In temperate estuaries, sea grasses are the predominant plants below the low tide marks. Like all true plants, these grasses produce flowers, pollen, and seeds. Once a year, thousands of underwater flowers release pollen that floats in the water, transported from one plant to another by waves and currents. After pollination, fertilized eggs mature into seeds that float away from the parent plants, sink, and start new beds of grass. Sea grasses can spread asexually by sending out runners called rhizomes that generate upright shoots. Rhizomes make it possible for sea grasses to quickly form large meadows on estuary floors.

The broad, flat blades of the sea grass strap weed (*Posidonia australis*) can be seen just below the surface of the water. Narrow-leaved eelgrasses (*Zostera capricorni*, *Zostera muelleri*, and *Heterozostera tasmanica*) prefer shallow water and can even be found on mudflats that are exposed to air. Paddle weeds (*Halophila ovalis* and *Halophila decipiens*), which have short, oval leaves, grow in solitary clumps instead of meadows like the other sea grasses. Depending on the climate, estuaries may contain other species such as turtle grass (*Thalassia testudinum*) and manatee grass (*Syringodium filiforme*).

Like all plants, sea grasses require plenty of light, so they are concentrated in the upper 6.6 feet (2 m) of the water column. Because they grow quickly and spread easily, underwater grasses produce a lot of food. Even though sea urchins and small crustaceans graze on them, most of the standing crop of grass dies and enters the detritus food chain. Bacteria and fungi feed on the grass, then invertebrates like crabs eat the partially digested grass blades along with the bacteria and fungi colonizing them. Fish and birds prey on the invertebrates.

As decomposers work on the grass, they generate dissolved organic matter (DOM) that leaches into water. This is an important source of food for other types of bacteria and several species of protozoans. Microbes that feed on DOM are eaten by small animals and protists, which in turn become food for other animals.

Although they are important producers of food, sea grasses play many other roles in the estuarine ecosystem. They host algae, green protists, and a variety of tiny, transparent animals on their blades and stems. Grasses also serve as habitats for fish and shellfish, protecting them from predators. In addition, they often act as nurseries where juveniles can find plenty of food and protection from predators. Because of sea grasses, there is both an abundance and diversity of fish in the estuarine system.

The presence of sea grasses impacts the size, shape, and depth of the estuary basin. Grass blades and stems slow down the rate at which water flows through the system. When water slows, suspended matter, including soil or organic material, settles. In this way sea grasses help build up, and cement together, the estuary floor.

In tropical climates, mangroves carry out many of the roles of sea grasses in more temperate zones. Mangroves are much larger plants than grasses; a mature mangrove tree can reach heights of 26.2 to 32.8 feet (8 to 10 m). Mangroves are never completely submerged; only their root systems are underwater. Roots are often covered in anoxic mud of the estuary or tidal marsh floor. To live and reproduce in such a difficult environment, mangroves display several unique adaptations.

Differences in Terrestrial and Aquatic Plants

Even though plants that live in water look dramatically different from terrestrial plants, the two groups have a lot in common. Both types of plants capture the Sun's energy and use it to make food from raw materials. In each case, the raw materials required include carbon dioxide, water, and minerals. The differences in these two types of plants are adaptations to their specific environments.

Land plants are highly specialized for their lifestyles. They get their nutrients from two sources: soil and air. It is the job of roots to absorb water and minerals from the soil, as well as hold the plant in place. Essential materials are transported to cells in leaves by a system of tubes called vascular tissue. Leaves are in charge of taking in carbon dioxide gas from the atmosphere for photosynthesis. Once photosynthesis is complete, a second set of vascular tissue carries the food made by the leaves to the rest of the plant. Land plants are also equipped with woody stems and branches that hold them upright so that they can receive plenty of light.

Marine plants, called macroalgae or seaweeds, get their nutrients, water, and dissolved gases from seawater. Since water surrounds the entire marine plant, these dissolved nutrients simply diffuse into each cell. For this reason, marine plants do not have vascular tissue to accommodate pho-

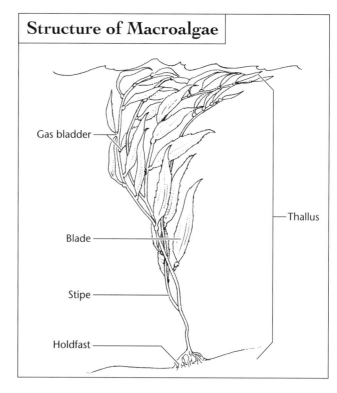

Structure of Macroalgae

Gas bladder

Thallus

Blade

Stipe

Holdfast

Fig. 2.3   The body, or thallus, of a macroalga is made up of leaflike blades, stemlike stipes, and rootlike holdfasts. Gas bladders on the stipes and blades help hold the plant near the top of the water column.

tosynthesis or to carry its products to each cell. In addition, marine plants do not need support structures because they are held up by the buoyant force of the water. Since water in the ocean is always moving, the bodies of marine plants are flexible, permitting them to go with that movement. Some marine plants secrete mucus to make their surfaces slick, further reducing their drag or resistance to water movement. Mucus also helps keep animals from eating them.

A plant that grows on land is described with terms such as *leaf, stem,* and *root.* Seaweeds are made up of different components, which are shown in Figure 2.3. The parts of seaweed that look like leaves are termed *blades,* or fronds. Some are equipped with small, gas-filled sacs, or *bladders,* that help keep them afloat and close to the sunlight. The gases in these bladders are usually nitrogen, argon, and oxygen. The stemlike structures of macroalgae are referred to as *stipes.* A root-shaped mass, the *holdfast,* anchors seaweeds but does not absorb nutrients like true roots do. Together, the blades, stipes, and holdfast make up the body, or *thallus,* of the macroalgae. Thalli take on many different forms, including tall and branched or thin and flat.

Since they grow in soft, shifting sediment, mangroves do not develop taproots like many terrestrial plants. Instead, their roots spread out broadly, some growing high on the trunk in order to support the plants. Mangrove trees also send out roots that rise vertically from the water to take in oxygen.

The amount of salt water that mangroves can endure would kill most other vascular plants. Mangroves have developed a variety of ways to regulate the amount of salt in their tissues. Some species simply exclude salt, blocking its transport into cells. These types of trees have special tissues on their submerged lower limbs and roots that act as barriers to protect them from salt intrusion. The stilted mangrove (*Rhizophora apiculata*) is capable of keeping 90 percent of the salt out of its tissues by exclusion. Other species, like the gray mangrove (*Avicennia marina*), excrete salt through glands on the surfaces of their leaves. When the leaves fall off the tree, the salt goes with them. Another mangrove technique for getting rid of salt is to concentrate it in old flowers, bark, or fruits. The loss of these plant parts helps lower salt levels.

To reproduce, terrestrial vascular plants form seeds that fall to the ground and germinate. For the mangroves, seed germination is more complex because the ground around them is covered with salt water and oxygen-poor sediment. To solve this problem, these plants use a unique reproductive strategy. Seeds of the mangroves stay on the trees longer than those of most vascular plants, giving them time to mature from the seed to the seedling stage. While on the parent tree, seedlings store more nutrients than simple seeds. By stocking up on food, seedlings are ready for a short season of extremely rapid growth once they find a suitable location. If these well-developed seedlings fall from the limbs of the parent trees when the tide is out, they land in the mud and quickly take root. If they fall into the water during high tide, they are washed out to a new location, and they establish a new plant there.

Living mangrove leaves are rarely grazed on by herbivores because they are coated with a distasteful, waxy material that helps them conserve water. However, detritivores are able to digest the covering, releasing the nutrients within. In this way, the fallen leaves and fruits of mangroves supply plant material to the detrital food chain.

Like sea grass roots, mangrove roots slow down the rate at which sediment-laden water swirls around the shore, so the soil it is carrying settles. By trapping and holding soil, mangrove roots help stabilize and expand shorelines. The roots also provide shade, hiding places, and food for animals. Many species of animals spend part of their lives among the roots, especially fish and invertebrates like oysters.

In many temperate zones, various species of cord grass (*Spartina*), shown in the lower color insert on page C-1, are the primary producers of the salt marsh. *Spartina* is one of the few plants that can live with its roots submerged in brackish water. Adaptations for its living conditions include narrow, tough blades that few animals can eat and glands that secrete excess salt. Like mangrove and sea grass, living *Spartina* is not an important source of food for animals. Dead *Spartina* is the fuel of the salt marsh detritus food chain.

Conclusion

Estuaries, salt marshes, and tidal flats are some of the most productive environments in the world. Regular flooding with nutrient-enriched water supports lush stands of sea grass, cord grass, and mangroves, as well as large populations of diatoms. In addition, green, red, and brown species of macroalgae grow where they can find suitable, firm substrates. Unlike most systems, the majority of energy captured in plants is not moved into the animal populations by the grazing of herbivores. Instead, bacteria and fungi break down dead plant matter that becomes food for small animals.

Sea grasses grow quickly in temperate estuaries, forming underwater meadows where young animals can hide, feed, and grow. Cord grass, a tough, spike-bladed plant, helps trap sediments and provides homes for hundreds of species of animals. In the tropics, mangrove roots create similar environments.

On the tidal flats, diatoms and blue-green algae spread across the tops of the sediments during low tides. When tides are in and the tidal flats are inundated with seawater, these microbes migrate below the surface of the sediment to protect themselves from the energy of moving water. When the tide is out, they move back atop the sediments, where they carry out photosynthesis. Diatoms help stabilize the sediments by producing sticky mucus that glues soil particles together and reduces erosion.

The food chains supported by estuarine producers are extremely successful. As a result of the energy captured by cyanobacteria, diatoms, macroalgae, and vascular plants, estuaries support as many different kinds of living things as coral reefs and rain forests. As a group, estuarine plants are some of the most productive in the world.

3

Sponges, Cnidarians, and Worms
The Saltwater Wetland's Simplest Animals

Animals, multicellular organisms that are *motile,* or able to move around, make up an immense kingdom. Included in this group are tiny life forms that can only be seen under microscopes, behemoths that reach lengths of more than 100 feet (30.5 m), and animals of all intermediate sizes. Scientists divide the members of the animal kingdom into two groups: *vertebrates* and *invertebrates.* Vertebrates, animals with backbones, include humans and many organisms with which humans are familiar, such as fish, frogs, lizards, birds, and dogs. Invertebrates are animals without backbones, such as snails, worms, jellyfish, crabs, and lobsters. They are generally smaller and less complex than vertebrates. Of the two groups of organisms, the invertebrates are by far the largest.

To facilitate the study of a group of organisms of such staggering size, invertebrates can arbitrarily be placed in two groups: simple and complex. The simpler organisms are the sponges, cnidarians, and worms. More complex invertebrates include mollusks, arthropods, and echinoderms.

A multicellular organism, like an animal, has more complicated physiology than a protist or moneran. Single-celled life-forms are able to take in oxygen and food directly from the environment through cell membranes. In the bodies of multicellular organisms, millions of cells are isolated from the environment. To service these cells, animals have developed body systems.

The respiratory system brings oxygen into an animal's body and takes carbon dioxide away. Cells of animals need oxygen to carry out the chemical reactions that change food to energy. Without oxygen, cells quickly run out of energy and die. Most estuarine invertebrates get oxygen from the brackish water that surrounds them. *Gills,* organs in the respiratory system of several marine invertebrates and fish, are made of thin sheets of tissue, each of which is equipped with thousands of tiny blood vessels. The tissues of gills are highly folded, packing a large surface area into a small space. As water flows over gills, oxygen dissolved in it diffuses into the blood stream. At the same time, carbon dioxide, a waste product of metabolism that is dissolved in the blood, is carried out of the body.

The respiratory system works in conjunction with the circulatory system, which distributes oxygen to the cells. The circulatory system also carries food molecules to cells and removes their metabolic wastes. To prepare the nutrients for delivery to cells, the digestive system takes food into the body and breaks it down. All of these body systems are run and coordinated by the nervous system. Some of the other body systems include the muscular system, which makes it possible for an animal to move; the integumentary system, which includes skin and other external tissues; and the excretory system that removes wastes.

Sponges in the Estuary

Sponges are primitive animals that lack complex tissues and organs. All of the body functions in a sponge are carried out by individual cells instead of by systems. Anatomically, sponges are made of only two layers of cells, an outer *epidermis* and an inner *gastrodermis*, as shown in Figure 3.1. Sandwiched between

Fig. 3.1   The epidermis (1) of a sponge is filled with tiny pores called porocytes (2). Amoebocytes (3) move around the sponge carrying food to cells. Water enters the sponge through an incurrent pore (4), flows into the central cavity, and exits through the osculum (5). Spicules (6) lend support to the sponge's body wall. Choanocytes (7) lash their flagella in the central cavity to keep water moving through the sponge and to gather bits of food that are suspended in the water. The mesoglea (8) is a jellylike matrix located between the epidermis and the cells that line the central cavity.

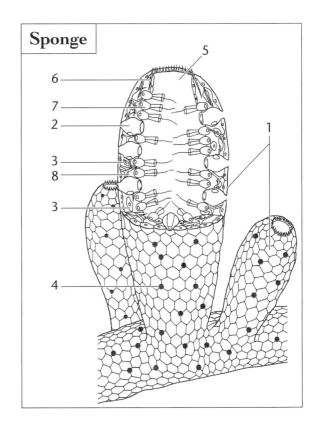

Sponge

these two is a jellylike layer, the mesoglea. For support, the bodies of sponges contain small, mineralized needles called *spicules* or tough protein fibers of spongin.

In a sponge, amoeba-like cells crawl through the mesoglea and both cell layers, carrying out many of the functions that are performed by tissues and organs in higher animals. When food is digested, amoeba-like cells pick up the nutrient molecules and share them with other sponge cells. Some of their other jobs include collecting and removing waste products as well as arranging the spicules in their proper places.

Sponges feed on tiny food particles that are captured by specialized collar cells, or *chaonocytes,* lining the gastrodermis. Each chaonocyte, equipped with a long, whiplike *flagellum,* helps create currents of water by lashing its flagellum back and forth. As a result, water continously flows into the sponge through tiny pores in the epidermis, then moves through the gastrovascular cavity and out one or more openings called oscula. As water flows past them, chaonocytes grab the food particles that are suspended in it.

Adult sponges are *sessile* organisms that spend all of their time in one place. The size and shape of an adult sponge varies with species as well as location. In estuary systems, many are low-growing, forming crusts or films over hard substrates like rock. A few species grow taller and take on the shapes of vases or fingers.

Sexually, sponges are *hermaphrodites,* organisms that are capable of producing both male and female sex cells. When signaled to do so by the climate and lunar phases, specialized sex cells in sponges transform into eggs and sperm. Sperm are discharged into the water, travel to another sponge, and enter it through the pores. Fertilization occurs inside the sponge that receives the sperm. In some species, both eggs and sperm are released, and they unite in the water instead of inside the sponge. The zygotes that result from fertilization become free-swimming *larvae* that eventually settle to the bottom, attach to the substrate, and grow into adult sponges. A sponge can also reproduce asexually by forming buds, small organisms that grow at the base of the parent sponge. When buds are mature, they separate from the parent and live independently. In addition, if a sponge is torn apart by waves, each part can develop into a new organism.

Several species of sponges are found in the estuarine environment, many of which are colorful, although relatively small. The red volcano sponge (*Acarnus erithaceus*) is easy to find because of its bright orange or scarlet color. This small sponge, which grows to 1.4 to 1.6 inches (4 to 6 cm) in diameter and 1.6 to 3.5 inches (6 to 9 cm) in length, is spotted with numerous, closely spaced oscula.

Two sponges that are similar in name and appearance are crumb-of-bread sponge (*Halichondria bowerbanki*) and bread crumb sponge (*Halichondria panicea*). Resembling bits of bread, as their names suggest, these sponges thrive best in sediment-rich sections of the estuary. A crumb-of-bread sponge colony, which grows up to 9.8 inches (25 cm) across and may be 4.7 inches (12 cm) tall, has a smooth surface, large oscula, and flattened, tassel-like branches. In warm weather, the sponge is beige or tan, but when temperatures cool it changes to tones of gray or yellow. During spawning season, the entire mass transforms into spectacular shades of yellow-orange.

Bread crumb sponge may develop chimneylike oscula across its surface or oscula at the ends of its tasseled branches. The sponge's branches can grow entwined in plants, animals, or rocks on the substrate. In places that are well sheltered from waves, bread crumb sponge attaches to substrates and produces colonies that span several feet. Most of the year, this beige- or cream-colored sponge can also be found on the flattened blades of red algae.

Adocia, a pale lavender sponge that grows in a flat form across substrates, produces tiny oscula on raised collars that are only 0.04 inch (1 mm) tall. *Aplysilla glacialis* is larger, reaching thicknesses of 0.08 inch (2 mm) and producing scattered oscula up to 2.4 inches (6 cm) tall. The bright, tomato-colored red-beard sponge (*Adocia*) grows to 8 inches (20 cm) in height with fingerlike projections. *Cliona*, a yellow boring sponge that secretes acid, bores into shellfish or rock structures. *Cliona* can be a serious predator of clams and oysters, reducing their populations substantially.

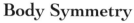

Body Symmetry

An important characteristic of the body plan of an animal is its symmetry. Symmetry refers to the equivalence in size and shape of sections of an animal's body. Most animals exhibit body symmetry, but a few species of sponges are asymmetrical. If a plane were passed through the body of an asymmetrical sponge, slicing it in two, the parts would not be the same.

Some animals are radially symmetrical. Shaped like either short or long cylinders, these stationary or slow-moving organisms have distinct top and bottom surfaces but lack fronts and backs, heads or tails. A plane could pass through a radially symmetrical animal in several places to create two identical halves. Starfish, jellyfish, sea cucumbers, sea lilies, and sand dollars are a few examples of radially symmetrical animals.

The bodies of most animals are bilaterally symmetrical, a form in which a plane could pass through the animal only in one place to divide it into two equal parts. The two halves of a bilaterally symmetrical animal are mirror images of each other. Bilateral symmetry is associated with animals that move around. The leading part of a bilaterally symmetrical animal's body contains sense organs such as eyes and nose. Fish, whales, birds, snakes, and humans are all bilaterally symmetrical.

Scientists have special terms to describe the body of a bilaterally symmetrical animal, depicted in Figure 3.2. The head or front region is called the anterior portion and the opposite end, the hind region, is the posterior. The stomach or underside is the ventral side, and opposite that is the back, or dorsal, side. Structures located on the side of an animal are described as lateral.

Fig. 3.2   A sponge (a) is an asymmetrical animal. Starfish and jellyfish (b) are radially symmetrical; snails, turtles, and fish (c) are bilaterally symmetrical. In a bilaterally symmetrical animal, the head or front end is described as anterior and the tail end as posterior. The front or stomach side is ventral and the back or top side is dorsal. The sides of the animal are described as lateral.

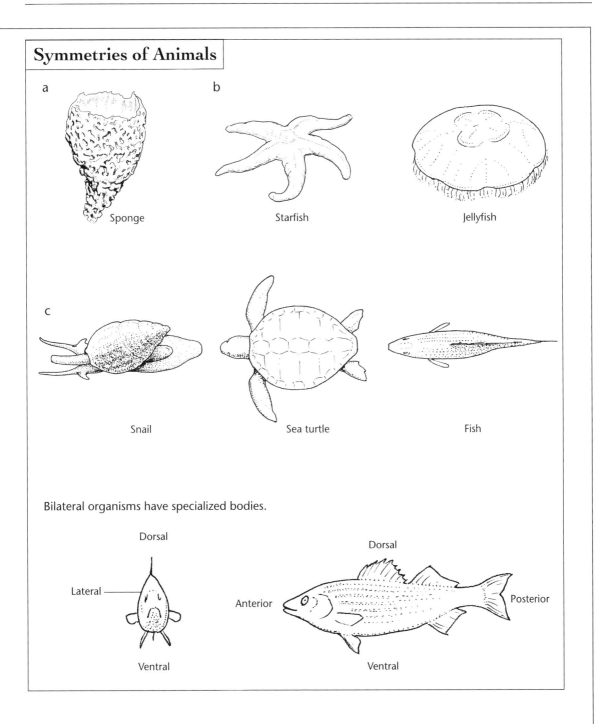

Symmetries of Animals

a

Sponge

b

Starfish

Jellyfish

c

Snail

Sea turtle

Fish

Bilateral organisms have specialized bodies.

Dorsal

Lateral

Ventral

Dorsal

Anterior

Posterior

Ventral

Cnidarians

For most people, the best-known cnidarians are the jellyfish. This group of invertebrates also includes lesser-known organisms such as hydrozoans and anemones. Of the three types, anemones are most common in estuaries.

Cnidarians are animals with simple, saclike bodies that can exist in two forms: polyps or medusae, as shown in Figure 3.3. The polyp is a vase-shaped sac in which the mouth of the organism is facing up. The medusa is just the opposite; a bell shape in which the mouth is on the underside of the body.

The cnidarian body is more complex than the body of a sponge, although still relatively simple. A cnidarian has only one opening, the mouth, which takes in food as well as expels waste products. The mouth is ringed with tentacles that can vary in number and length. The body wall is made of two layers, the epidermis and endodermis, with a jellylike mesoglea between them.

For quick cell-to-cell communication, the body of a cnidarian is equipped with a simple network of nerves. The nerve net connects to specialized cells, *cnidocytes*, on the tentacles

Fig. 3.3   Cnidarians have two body plans: either a vase-shaped polyp (a) or a bell-shaped medusa (b). Each plan is equipped with tentacles (1), a gastrovascular cavity (2), and a single body opening, the mouth (3).

Cnidarian Body Plans

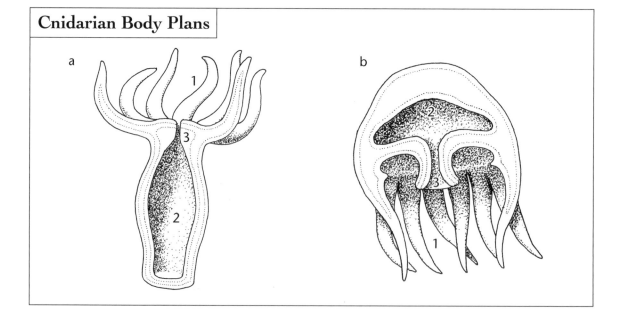

that play roles in defense and in capturing food. Each cnido-cyte contains a *nematocyst*, a barb attached to a long filament that can be fired at prey as well as at a predator. When triggered, a nematocyst uncoils and shoots out a barbed tip. In some species, the tips contain poisons that can paralyze or kill prey, and in others, they are covered with sticky mucus. Once an item is snared, tentacles move it through the cnidarian's mouth and into the gastrovascular cavity. There, enzymes break it down, and cells in the gut cavity absorb the nutrients. Undigested parts are expelled through the mouth.

Anemones are cnidarians that spend their entire lives in the polyp form. The body of an anemone is a thick column with two distinct ends. The upper end, or the oral disk, contains the mouth, an opening surrounded by a ring of tentacles. The other end of the animal, the pedal disk, attaches to hard substrates with a suction cup–like action. Some anemones secrete a sticky adhesive to help hold them in place. Although the animals are classified as sessile, anemones have some strategies for moving around. They can shuffle across the substrate very slowly on their pedal disks, somersault on their tentacles from place to place, or inflate their bodies with air and float to a new location.

Anemones occur in colonies or singly. As a colony, anemones are able to conserve more moisture than one organism can do alone. For that reason, colonial species suffer less stress than solitary ones when the tide is out. Both colonial and solitary organisms may use their tentacles to pick up tiny bits of shell or rock, which they place on their tentacles like hats for protection from the Sun and drying. This technique also helps camouflage them from predators.

Some species of anemones contain one or more symbiotic organisms, usually simple green algae or dinoflagellates, protists that contain chlorophyll. As a group, one-celled autotrophs like dinoflagellates that live in the tissues of plants or animals are known as *zooxanthellae*. By living together in a *symbiotic* relationship, both the host animal and its autotrophic guests benefit. The protists supply food and oxygen for their host who, in return, protects the autotrophs from predators and provides a place to live that gets plenty of exposure to sunlight.

The aggregate green anemone (*Anthopleura elegantissima*) has a green body, pink-tipped tentacles, and radiating lines on the oral disk. Aggregate green anemones may occur as solitary individuals or as colonies referred to as aggregates. The solitary form usually grows to 6 inches (15 cm) in diameter, while individuals within aggregates are smaller, only 0.8 to 2 inches (2 to 5 cm) wide. The anemone may strategically cover its mouth and tentacles with bits of shell and stone for protection.

The aggregate green anemone contains both green algae and dinoflagellate symbionts, but like all anemones, it can also catch food with its tentacles. Prey, which includes small bug-like copepods, isopods, and amphipods, are either stung by nematocysts or ensnared in sticky mucus on the tentacles. Once subdued, the anemone pushes the prey through its mouth and into the gastrovascular cavity.

Anthopleura elegantissima can reproduce sexually and asexually. In the sexual phase, it releases both eggs and sperm during the summer months. Eggs are fertilized in the gastric cavity, and the young emerge from the mouth as free-swimming larvae. After a short time, they settle to the bottom to grow into adult anemones. Asexual reproduction occurs by longitudinal fission, a process in which the organism splits down the middle to form two individuals. Fission creates clones of anemones that form aggregates. If two different aggregates of anemones meet, individuals on the edges fight with each other using their tentacles until a border eventually develops between the feuding groups.

The giant green anemone can grow to almost 1 foot (30 cm) in height and 9 inches (25 cm) in diameter but is usually smaller. The column of this colossal species varies from green to brown, depending on how much sunlight it receives, and its tentacles are green, blue, or white. Like its cousin the aggregate green anemone, the giant green anemone's color is due to zooxanthellae. The giant green anemone does not undergo fission but relies only on sexual reproduction. Mussels that have become detached from the substrates are its preferred food, but the anemone will also eat crabs, urchins, and small fish. Larvae of the giant green anemone often settle near a mussel bed.

Some researchers believe that giant green anemones may live 300 to 500 years. The anemones do not seem to age like most animals; rather, they thrive in a youthful condition until they are killed by accident, disease, or predators. The primary enemies of this long-lived giant are carnivorous snails, which eat the tentacles; sea spiders that suck the juices out of the column; and some sea stars that eat the anemone.

Many other types of anemones are found in estuaries, and species vary by geographical location. The red and green or painted anemone (*Telia [Urticina] crassicornis*), shown in the upper color insert on page C-2 prefers areas where the salinity is about half that of ocean water. An olive or greenish gray trunk streaked with bright red marks and thick, blunt tentacles ringed in white make this anemone easy to identify. The painted anemone can grow to 5 inches (12.7 cm) tall and reach widths of 3 inches (7.6 cm).

The common sea anemone (*Metridium senile*) is yellow brown to pink and grows 3.9 inches (10 cm) tall. The pallid sea anemone (*Diadumine leucolena*) can be found living under eelgrass, while the transparent burrowing sea anemone (*Haloclava producta*) hides in the sediment with only its tentacles exposed.

Unlike the anemones, which exist as polyps, jellyfish are cnidarians that spend their entire lives in the medusa stage. Most live off the coast and in deep water but may appear seasonally in bays, estuaries, and inlets. Jellyfish are

Spawning and Brooding

For sexual reproduction to take place, male and female cells must come together. Many marine species spawn, or discharge one or both of their sex cells into the water. For this strategy to be successful, eggs and sperm must be released at the same time, which is why spawning usually occurs once a year at a specific time. Animals are cued to release gametes by specific environmental factors, such as the Moon's phase, length of daylight, or temperature.

The alternative strategy to spawning is brooding. Animals that brood release sperm into the water, while eggs remain within the mother. Sperm swim around until they find a female, enter her body, and fertilize the eggs. Eggs are brooded within the mother's body until time for them to hatch.

Fertilized eggs that are brooded have the advantage of protection from predators during development. In comparison, eggs fertilized in the water column or on the seafloor are at high risk from predators. For this reason, animals that brood their developing eggs only produce small numbers of gametes, while those that spawn discharge hundreds of thousands of gametes, a strategy that ensures that a few of the resulting offspring will survive until adulthood.

most likely to be spotted in estuaries when the salinity of the estuary water is about the same as the ocean's water.

One of the few species that may spend its entire life among the estuarine eelgrass beds is the stalked jellyfish (*Haliclystus*). Looking more like a flower than a jellyfish, this organism attaches to the substrate by a stalk on top of which the medusa is flipped upside down, with the mouth facing up. The "petals" of the "flower" are eight lobes of the medusa, each tipped with club-like tentacles. In *Haliclystus auricula*, each lobe ends in hundreds of tentacles. This very small jellyfish, which grows to 1.75 inches (3.1 cm) in height, feeds on worms and other small shore animals.

The upside-down jellyfish (*Cassiopeia xamachana*), shown in the lower color insert on page C-2, is found in mangrove estuarine systems. The presence of zooxanthellae in the jellyfish's tissues give this 12-inch (30-cm) cnidarian a greenish brown color. At a very young age, this animal rests its dorsal side, or bell, on the estuary bottom where it looks very much like an anemone. The bell acts like a giant suction cup, holding the jellyfish in place. The upside-down jellyfish extends its frilly, brown tentacles up into the water column to capture food, a supplement to the supplies made by the algae living in its body.

Unlike other species of jellyfish, the upside-down jellyfish lacks a centrally located mouth. Instead, hundreds of tiny mouth openings are found along the fringe of its bell. However, reproduction in the upside-down jellyfish is typical of other jellyfish species. After the female produces eggs, she holds them until the male releases sperm. Then she collects the male's sperm with her tentacles and fertilizes her eggs. Hatchlings develop into larvae that become tiny polyps. Each polyp produces clones of itself, all of which become swimming jellyfish.

During the late spring and summer, the moon jelly (*Aurelia aurita*) may visit estuarine systems. The moon jelly's gray-white, translucent bell can reach 10 inches (25 cm) in width. Short, fringed tentacles and four reproductive organs arranged in a cloverleaf pattern make these jellyfish easy to identify. The lion's mane jellyfish (*Cyanea capillata*), in

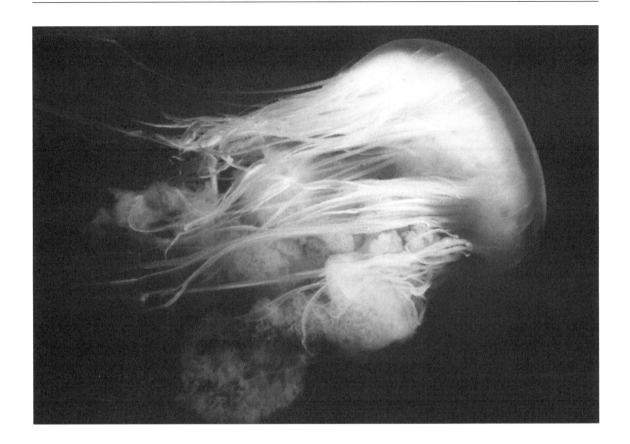

Figure 3.4, may also appear. About the same size as the moon jelly, the color of the lion's mane jellyfish varies with age and changes from shades of reds to pinks. Flowing, mane-like, yellow-orange tentacles hanging around its mouth earned this jellyfish its name.

Fig. 3.4   The lion's mane jellyfish is named for its bright golden color. (Courtesy of Kip Evans, NOAA)

Comb Jellies

Comb jellies, shown in Figure 3.5, are jellyfish-like animals that have eight rows of "combs," or large, fused *cilia*, along their sides. The cilia beat together to propel the animals through the water, but some animals also flap their bodies to improve their swimming. In some species, two long tentacles hang down from the bell, while in others, no tentacles are present. Because they lack stinging cells, comb jellies are not

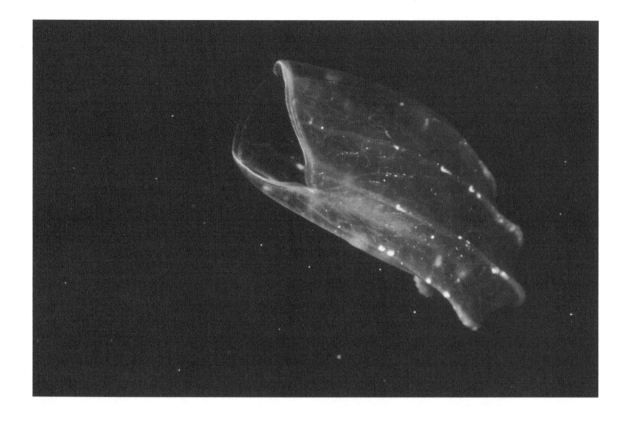

Fig. 3.5 Although this comb jelly resembles a jellyfish, it belongs to the group of animals known as ctenophores. (Courtesy of OAR/National Undersea Research Program (NURP), NOAA)

classified as cnidarians. Instead, scientists place them in a separate group, the ctenophores. Short tentacles and cilia move food particles to the mouth. Many types of comb jellies give off bioluminescent light when disturbed.

The common southern comb jelly, or the sea walnut (*Mnemiopsis leidyi*), is most likely to be found in the estuary during the summer. Growing to lengths of two to three inches (5 to 7.6 cm), two long lobes hang down below its transparent body. Sea walnuts float around with their lobes spread so that sticky cells inside their bodies help capture small prey, like larvae of fish and shellfish that are swimming in plankton. When disturbed, the animals produce a blue-green bioluminescent glow and flap their lobes for a speedy escape.

The sea gooseberry (*Pleurobrachia pileus*), another comb jelly, is smaller than the sea walnut, reaching lengths of only 0.75 inch (2 cm). Fringed tentacles that hang longer than the body help it trap food. This animal is most likely to be found in the estuary during the winter months.

Bioluminescence

A few organisms have the ability to bioluminesce, or produce their own light. In the marine environment, light-producers include bacteria, phytoplankton, invertebrates, and fish. Bioluminescent light results from a chemical reaction that occurs within cells. A protein, luciferin, reacts with an enzyme, luciferase, in the presence of oxygen. A molecule of luciferin can only be used one time, and in most organisms new luciferin must be provided for each reaction. In some cases, luciferin and luciferase are chemically bound to one another as a large molecule called a photoprotein. Calcium and some other ions are able to trigger photoproteins to react. Most of the energy of the reaction is released as light, with very little wasted in the form of heat.

Scientists hypothesize that light-generating reactions must be important to the survival of organisms that use them because the very act of making light consumes up to 10 percent of their energy. No one knows for certain the purpose of light production, but four theories have been suggested. Light may help organisms evade their predators, attract their prey, communicate with others of their own species, or advertise. An anglerfish, which lives in deep water, where little or no light penetrates, attracts prey by dangling a glowing, lurelike appendage near its mouth. When an unsuspecting fish comes by to inspect it, the anglerfish lunges forward and engulfs it.

Flashlight fish have patches under their eyes that are filled with light-producing bacteria. The fish can control the amount of light emitted from the patches by raising or lowering lids that can cover them. These animals may use blinking signals as a form of communication, similar to the flashes produced by fireflies. A dinoflagellate, *Noctiluca,* glows when a wave or boat jostles the water, or when a fish swims nearby. The light it releases may help confuse predators swimming in its midst.

The amount of light produced by bioluminescence is significant. Even though the glow from a single dinoflagellate lasts only 0.1 seconds, it is visible to the human eye. Larger organisms, like jellyfish, emit greater quantities of light. Jellyfish and other large organisms may glow for tens of seconds.

Most of the light produced by living things is blue. Underwater blue light can travel farther than any other color, so light produced in shades of blue is carried the greatest possible distance. In addition, most marine organisms are adapted to see shades of blue but are blind to other colors. An exception to this rule is a fish known as loosejaw that gives off, and is capable of seeing, red light. Humans cannot see the glow of loosejaws because the shade of red it emits is close to the infrared portion of the electromagnetic spectrum. This fish may be better camouflaged than any other bioluminescent organism since it produces a light that helps it see its own species and possibly its prey, while it cannot be seen by other organisms.

Worms

On the bottoms of estuaries, tidal flats, and salt marshes, populations of worms are large. The burrowing activity of sediment-dwelling worms helps aerate the soil and bring buried nutrients to the surface. In addition, worms are key components of the estuarine food chain. In the estuary, worms fall into two primary groups: flat worms and polychaetes, or segmented, worms. Of the two, flat worms are simpler.

Marine flatworms are thin animals whose bodies lack segments and appendages. They move by gliding across substrates on hairlike cilia. The digestive system of a flatworm has only one opening that handles food intake and waste expulsion. A flatworm feeds with a muscular tube called a pharynx, which it extends onto its meal. Digestive enzymes from the tube break down the food to a slushy consistency so that it can

Worm Comparisons

Segmented worms are much more advanced and complex than flatworms. The digestive systems of flatworms are one-way tubes sandwiched between two body walls. However, segmented worms have a space between their two body walls called the body cavity, or coelom, that represents an important evolutionary advance, one that provides a place for the body's internal organs. In segmented worms, organs are held in their proper places inside the coelom by a membrane, the peritoneum.

All animals with coeloms are equipped with one set of muscles around the body wall and another set around the digestive system. The body wall muscles help the animal move about, while the digestive system muscles push food along the digestive tract. In contrast, flatworms have only one set of muscles in their body wall, and these muscles must carry out both functions.

Segmentation is an advance in animal evolution because segmented animals can increase in size by adding more body portions. In addition, segments can become specialized to carry out certain jobs. Flatworms are therefore limited in size as well as in the degree of specialization they can reach because they lack segments.

A flatworm gets oxygen and loses carbon dioxide by simple diffusion through the epidermis. Segmented worms have more complex gas exchange systems. Oxygen diffuses through the skin into blood vessels. Blood then carries oxygen to cells deep in

be sucked into the body. Most species of flatworms are carnivores that prey on small invertebrates and protozoans.

Flatworms may reproduce in several ways. Some divide asexually by fission, producing two identical offspring. Other species have all-female populations whose eggs develop without fertilization. Most types of flatworms are hermaphrodites so are capable of producing both eggs and sperm. During mating seasons, worms exchange gametes in order to cross-fertilize.

Tentacle-like folds of tissue on the posterior end of a marine flatworm gather information about the environment. The tissues can detect chemicals in the water and help worms navigate as well as find food. Two to six pairs of light-sensitive eyespots in the same area help the animal to avoid predators.

Two-colored flatworms (*Pseudoceros bicolor*) may grow 1 inch (2.5 cm) long. Mating pairs of hermaphrodites

---

the worm's body, while it picks up carbon dioxide and carries it out of the body. The blood of segmented worms contains hemoglobin, an iron-containing compound that attracts oxygen and binds to it. Blood with hemoglobin is capable of carrying 50 times more oxygen than blood that lacks the molecule. Near the head of the segmented worm, five pairs of muscular vessels or hearts squeeze rhythmically to keep blood circulating through the worm's body.

Segmented worms have much more advanced digestive systems than flatworms do. A flatworm has one opening, a mouth, for food and wastes. A segmented worm has two openings, a mouth at one end and an anus at the other. The mouth opens to an esophagus that leads to a muscular pharynx. Food travels from the pharynx to the crop where it can be stored temporarily before entering the gizzard, an organ that grinds it. From there, food goes to the intestine, the site of digestion. Digested nutrients enter the bloodstream, and waste materials are expelled through the anus. Segmented worms also have special organs called nephridia that remove nitrogen wastes from blood and excrete those wastes through tiny openings in the body wall.

The evolutionary advancements from flatworms to segmented worms are reflected in other animals such as mollusks and crustaceans, as well as in vertebrates. The segmented worms, although still evolutionarily simple, provided the groundwork from which further advancement evolved.

cross-fertilize when one of the worms stabs the other with its stylet-type penis. Sperm are injected into the body of the recipient and travel from the point of injection to the ovaries. Stylets are sharp and cause serious injuries, although most heal quickly.

Segmented worms, the polychaetes, are more numerous than flatworms. The tubular bodies of polychaetes are divided into sections or segments. Hairlike bristles called setae are located on the body surface. Some segmented worms also have parapodia, or foot-like appendages, that can vary in structure from small bumps to complex projections. Marine polychaetes are either free-swimming or sedentary. The swimming polychaetes have more prominent parapodia than the crawling species.

Unlike flatworms, sexes are separate in polychaetes During mating, eggs and sperm are discharged into the water. These sex cells unite to form zygotes that develop into larvae. After swimming in the shallow water for a short time, larvae settle to the bottom, where growth is completed.

The free swimming, or errant, species of polychaetes spend time wandering in the environment searching for food. Their bodies are long and slender, with little variation from head to tail. In some species, the head end possesses structures that are specialized for feeding, such as a proboscis and jaws. Some animals also have gills around the head. Errant worms such as bloodworms and sand worms build tubes where they rest.

The pale skin of bloodworms (*Glycera*) permits their red body fluids to show through, giving them their names. These 15-inch (38.1-cm) long worms have tapered heads equipped with four antennae. Compared to some polychaete species, bloodworms are poor swimmers. Their small, fleshy parapodia help them crawl across, or burrow into, the sediment.

A bloodworm has a large proboscis that is armed with four retractable black fangs. These animals are most abundant on the middle of tidal flats, where they can use their toothed proboscis to quickly bury themselves into the ground. Because bloodworms are tolerant of low oxygen levels and fluctuating salinity, they are well adapted for life in estuarine sediment.

A group of polychaetes collectively known as clam worms (*Nereis*) have well-developed parapodia and head appendages. The sand worm (*Nereis vexillosa*) is an estuarine polychaete whose long, gray body reflects iridescent reds, greens, and blues.

Adults may reach lengths of 6 inches (30 cm). Each segment of the worm is equipped with setae and a pair of parapodia.

Sand worms are omnivores that use their pharynx and pincerlike jaws to consume several kinds of food. During the day, sand worms hide in mucus-lined burrows in the sediment. At night, they emerge to find prey, usually small crustaceans or mollusks. The worms also scavenge on dead animals they find, or they scrape up meals of algae with their radulae.

When sand worms reach sexual maturity, their appearance undergoes a drastic change. In both sexes, the posterior segments turn red and swell with gametes. The parapodia, which had been primarily used for walking, transform into swimming appendages. Cued by moon phases, male worms leave the mud and swim into the water. As they swim, the worms twist their bodies violently, an action that releases sperm. Male activity stimulates females to enter the water and release eggs. The adults, whose bodies are now empty husks, die.

Other polychaetes are described as sedentary because they stay in one place, waiting for food to come to them. Their bodies are often shorter than those of errant worms, with clearly defined regions. Sedentary polychaetes spend their lives in tubes or holes, so they have developed a variety of special adaptations for feeding and breathing in these niches. Most species consume plankton or other small material suspended in the water. In the estuary, some of the sedentary polychaetes include lugworms, bamboo worms, mud worms, and bristle worms.

The eight-inch (20-cm) long body of a lugworm (*Arenicola*) is divided into three regions. Both the head and tail lack appendages, but the thick trunk has bundles of setae and tufts of gills on each side. Lugworms dig U-shaped burrows with openings at both ends. A worm excavates its burrow by ingesting soil with its proboscis, then backing out of its burrow to discharge the dirt into a pile of casting by the door of its home. Lugworms feed on organic particles brought in by water flowing through their burrows.

Bamboo worms (*Clymenella*) look very much like the plants for which they are named. Their four- to six-inch (10- to 15.2-cm) long bodies are made up of only a few extended segments with sparse parapodia. Found below the low tide level in mixed sand and mud sediments, these worms are deposit feeders who consume soil to get at the organic matter and nutrients it contains. Each worm lives in a tube made of sand and mud.

Living in soft, mucus-lined tubes below the surface of estuarine sediment, mud worms (*Streblospio benedicti*) have paired, oar-shaped appendages on every body segment. Their heads are equipped with several sensory organs, including eyes and tentacles. The bodies of mud worms are reddish brown and the gills dark green. These sediment feeders eat mud and detritus that they capture in their feeding tentacles. Distribution of *Streblospio benedicti* in estuarine waters is determined by salinity levels. The species cannot tolerate low salinities, and population sizes decrease as salinity drops.

Bristle worms are also estuarine residents. *Capitella capitata* is a small bristle worm with an enlarged anterior end. Growing only 3.9 inches (10 cm) in length, its red body is extremely flexible but fragile. Using its proboscis, *Capitella capitata* burrows into the black mud of tidal flats and estuaries, where it can endure low oxygen levels. Another type of bristle worm is *Cirratulus cirratus*. This long, slender species has an orange or brownish red body that can grow to 4.7 inches (12 cm) in length and a blunt head with four to eight large black eyes on each side. *Cirratulus cirratus* lives in tubes in the soil with only its gills and feeding tentacles aboveground.

Conclusion

Animals are motile, multicellular organisms that get their nutrition by ingesting food. The invertebrate group, composed of animals without backbones, includes a large number of organisms. Of these, sponges, cnidarians, ctenophores, and worms are some of the simplest.

Sponges are primitive animals, lacking organized tissues, organs, and organ systems. To circulate water through their bodies, sponges use a chimney and flue system that pulls water into the animal through pores and sends it out through the osculum. As water travels through a sponge, specialized chaonocytes collect suspended food particles. Amoebocytes pick up the products of food digestion and distribute them to all the other cells in the sponge.

Most estuarine sponges are small animals that stand only a few inches tall, although they may form colonies that spread across large areas. Red volcano and red beard are two sponges that are relatively easy to spot because of their scarlet color. Crumb-of-bread sponge and bread crumb sponge, both aptly named, look like pieces of bread on the estuary floor. *Cliona* is a bright yellow sponge that bores holes into the shells of mollusks.

The body of a cnidarian is more complex than a sponge. Simple body systems, including the saclike digestive system and the nerve net, help coordinate body activities and maintain all of the cells. Cnidarians are animals that possess stinging cells for defense and to gather food. Many species host zooxanthellae such as dinoflagellates or unicellular green algae. Estuarine cnidarians include anemones, hydroids, and jellyfish.

Anemones are found on the estuary floor in relatively clear, shallow water. An anemone sits on its basal disc, with its tentacle-encircled oral disc facing up. Many species are left exposed to the air when the tide goes out, so to conserve water, they shade their bodies with pieces of shell and debris. Colonial species, like the aggregate green anemone, form large colonies of individuals by asexual reproduction. Solitary organisms, like the giant green anemone, red anemone, and common sea anemone, grow larger than their colonial peers. Occasionally anemones change positions by sliding on the basal disc, somersaulting, or floating to another location.

Both the stalked jellyfish and the upside-down jellyfish are sessile species that make their homes on the estuary floor. The stalked jellyfish resembles a flower growing from the substrate, with the stalk as the "flower" stem and the inverted medusa as the "petals." The upside-down jellyfish lacks a stalk and inverts its bell on the substrate floor, streaming its tentacles up into the water column to grasp for food. Captured prey are pushed through tiny mouth openings around the fringe of the bell. Despite their ability to capture prey, most of these jellyfish depend on zooxanthellae for nutrition.

Comb jellies look a lot like jellyfish but are classified as ctenophores. Even though their bodies have many of the same features as cnidarians, comb jellies lack stinging cells.

The sea walnut can be found in the estuary during summer months and is notable for the blue-green glow it radiates through bioluminescence.

Worms represent a large portion of the living organisms on the estuary floor. The simplest types, flatworms, possess digestive systems with only one opening for feeding and emptying waste material. Flatworms are equipped with sensory devices like eyespots and tentacle-like folds of tissue that detect chemicals in the water.

Polychaetes are worms whose bodies are divided into segments. Most have appendages for locomotion and respiration located on some or all of their segments. Polychaetes may be errant or sedentary. The errant species, like blood worms and sand worms, divide their time between resting inside their burrows and wandering the environment in search of food. Sedentary species such as lugworms, bamboo worms, mud worms and capitellids remain in their burrows full time and feed by filtering organic matter from soil and water. The roles of worms are extremely important in the ecosystem. Their burrowing activity aerates the soil and helps bring valuable nutrients to the surface.

4

Mollusks, Arthropods, and Echinoderms
Advanced Invertebrates of the Saltwater Wetland

Simple marine animals such as sponges, jellyfish, and worms make up only a portion of the invertebrate species found in estuarine systems. The estuary is also home to several groups of complex animals without backbones. Among these are mollusks, arthropods, and echinoderms.

The mollusks include animals such as snails, clams, and squid. Snails, which have one shell, feed by scraping up their food with a file-like tongue. Closely related to snails are the two-shelled mollusks, a group that includes mussels, oysters, and clams. Primarily filter feeders, members of this group spend most of their lives burrowed in the estuary floor. Squid and octopus, members of a third group of mollusks, share a lot of internal features with their cousins, even though they have very different body shapes and shells.

Arthropods, such as barnacles, shrimp, and crabs, are segmented animals whose bodies are covered with tough exterior skeletons that protect them from predators. Many arthropods are important consumers in the estuarine food web, preying upon smaller animals like mollusks and worms. Animals with spiny skin, the echinoderms, include sea stars, sea urchins, and sea cucumbers. Echinoderms possess incredible powers of regeneration that enable them to replace lost limbs or sections of their digestive systems. Most are slow-moving animals that get around on tiny tubular-shaped feet that act as suction cups.

Many of the complex invertebrates spend at least part of their lives in the plankton, the mass of tiny organisms floating in the water column. Plankton is made up of unicellular organisms as well as tiny plants and animals which are carried around in the sea by the energy of waves and tides. Those that can photosynthesize, such as diatoms and unicellular green algae, are collectively known as phytoplankton. The tiny heterotrophs, which include protists and small animals, are called zooplankton. Planktonic organisms are important sources of food for thousands of life-forms in the estuary.

Mollusks

The estuary provides an ideal home for several types of mollusks. The term *mollusk* literally means "soft-bodied," a name that describes the general anatomy of organisms in this large group. Mollusks are adapted for a wide variety of habitats and have evolved several body styles. In the estuarine system, two groups are easy to locate: gastropods, the snails and their relatives, and bivalves, the clams and other animals with two shells. Some cephalopods such as octopuses and squid are present, but in much smaller numbers.

All mollusks share some common traits. Each has a soft body that contains organ systems for circulation, respiration, reproduction, digestion, and excretion, as shown in Figure 4.1. A thin tissue, the *mantle,* covers the body. In some species the mantle secretes the shell as well as one or more defensive chemicals, like ink, mucus, or acid. A mollusk also possesses a muscular foot that is either used to cling to substrates or to provide locomotion. A large number of mollusks eat by scraping up food with *radulae,* muscular tongues that are coated with sharp, toothlike protrusions. These scraping organs can efficiently take in algae, animal tissue, or detritus. One group, the bivalves, are primarily filter feeders that trap and consume food particles that are suspended in water. Cephalopods are predators that feed on other types of mollusks and crustaceans.

Many mollusks are slow-moving animals whose soft bodies need protection from predators. For gastropods and bivalves, this protection comes from their shells. Their shells

Fig. 4.1   The organs and muscular foot of a bivalve are located between its two shells.

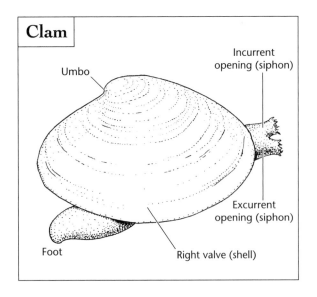

Clam

Umbo

Incurrent opening (siphon)

Excurrent opening (siphon)

Foot

Right valve (shell)

also serve other functions: They provide points of attachment for muscles and prevent drying of body tissues.

In all groups of mollusks, sexes are separate. Bivalves release their eggs and sperm into the water, and fertilization occurs there. In gastropods and cephalopods, internal fertilization, a process in which sperm are transferred to the body of the female, is the norm. Following fertilization, females deposit strings or cases of eggs on the sand, seaweed, or rocks. Zygotes develop into swimming larvae, most of which spend a few days or weeks in the plankton before metamorphosing into adult forms.

Gastropods

Many well-known estuarine mollusks are classified as gastropods, including snails, whelks, and drills. Most have one shell, although some species are shell-less. The head is equipped with sensory organs, including eyes, tentacles, and a mouth. Locomotion is provided by one large, flat foot located in the center of the body. Snails have spiral-shaped shells that contain and protect the animals' internal organs. In some species, an *operculum,* a flap or door that can close the shell, protects the occupant from danger.

The Asian mud snail (*Batillaria attramentaria*) crawls slowly over the mud of tidal flats, feeding on diatoms that live in the top layers of mud. Unlike most mollusks, the eggs of Asian mud snails do not develop into planktonic larvae. The adult female lays egg pouches in the mud that produce hatchlings that are very similar in body shape to the parents. Since this species lacks the swimming larval stage typical of most snails, its offspring do not disperse through the environment, and most young grow up in the same place they were born.

The pulmonate snail (*Melampus bidentatus*) prefers to live among grass blades in the high intertidal zone. Pulmonate snails have lungs and breathe air but are also capable of staying underwater indefinitely by breathing through their body surface. During the spring high tide, pulmonate snails release planktonic larvae that swim for two weeks before they are washed back into the high intertidal zone during the next spring tide. Once deposited, they mature into typical adult forms with light-colored shells that are striped with dark bands.

The eastern mud snail (*Ilyanassa obsoleta*) has a cone-shaped shell that grows to about one inch (2.5 cm) in length. The dark brown to black shell is crisscrossed with white lines, with small knobs marking the points at which the lines intersect. Eastern mud snails consume diatoms on tidal flats and salt marshes on the eastern U.S. coast, competing for both food and space with the California horned snail (*Cerithidea californica*). A heavy brown and white shell is an identifying characteristic of the California horned snail.

The marsh, or common, periwinkle (*Littorina irrorata*) is a whitish snail with red-brown spots on its shell and inside the shell's sharp, outer lip. Most of its life is spent on cord grass, where the snail moves up and down the plant stalks as the tide ebbs and flow, always staying just above the water.

In the invertebrate world, the marsh periwinkle, seen in the upper color insert on page C-3, has some unusual habits. Instead of feeding on plant material or preying on diatoms like many other snail species, it prefers to eat the fungi that infest cord grass. To encourage the growth of fungi, the periwinkles injure the grass blades, cutting furrows in them with their sharp radulae. As they work, marsh periwinkles also fertilize the furrows by depositing their feces, which contain fungal spores and nutrients, in the wounds. Once fungi have infected the grass, the snails move back in and feed on them. Grasses slashed by the marsh periwinkle develop fungal infections much faster than grasses that are not damaged. This type of fungal farming is rare, previously known in only a few species of insects.

The Atlantic oyster drill (*Urosalpinx cinerea*) is a snail that drills holes in oyster shells. Encased in an oval shell that is 1.2 inches (3 cm) long, this whitish-purple gastropod bores small, perfectly round holes into a variety of shelled invertebrates so it can eat their soft body parts. Before drilling with its radula, the snail secretes a chemical on its prey that softens the shell. When the hole is complete, the snail inserts its proboscis, a tubular feeding organ, spreads digestive enzymes on the prey, then sucks up the mushy body parts.

Bivalves

Bivalves are mollusks whose bodies are contained within two shells or valves. These valves hinge together on one side and are opened and closed by strong adductor muscles. Cockles, clams, mussels, oysters, and abalones are some of the bivalves found in the estuarine environment.

The soft body of a bivalve does not have a distinctive head or tail region. A large foot, located in the center of the body, can extend through the partially opened shells. Depending on the species, a bivalve can use its foot to grasp a substrate, burrow into the sand, or swim. In species that burrow, a section of the mantle is modified to form two siphons, tubes that extend from the body into the water to circulate water over the gills.

As filter feeders, bivalves depend on their gills to exchange gases with the water as well as trap bits of food. Water enters the mantle cavity through the inhalant siphon. Hairlike cilia and mucus cover the gills, which are located in the mantle cavity. Food particles in the water stick to the mucus on the gills, then are swept into the mouth by cilia. Indigestible particles exit through the exhalant siphon, creating a pile of silt around the bivalve. Bivalves must move a lot of water through their bodies to gather enough food to sustain them. An average-sized mussel can process 0.26 gallons (1 L) of water every hour.

The blue mussel (*Mytilus edulis*) is a typical gastropod; its blue-black shell is 1.9 inches (5 cm) long and shaped somewhat like an elongated triangle. Blue mussels occur in estuaries from temperate to Arctic regions. Most of their lives are spent in one spot, but occasionally they move a short distance to improve their positions in water currents. A mussel anchors its body to a substrate with byssus threads secreted by glands in the foot. After the threads are spun, they harden and hold the animal securely in place. To move, the mussel adjusts the lengths of existing threads and produces new ones. Byssus threads can also be used for defense, enabling mussels to disable predatory snails by tying them down.

Female blue mussels begin producing eggs at one year of age, releasing 5 to 12 million into the water during each spawning event. At the same time, males release sperm, which fertilize the eggs externally. Each fertilized egg develops into a trochophore larva, a minute organism whose midriff is belted in cilia. The trochophore matures into a veliger larva, which is distinguished by sail-shaped, cilia-bearing protrusions. After four to six weeks of larval development, the mussel attains a length of 0.01 inch (0.25 mm), at which time it changes into a juvenile form. The juvenile settles on the substrate and develops into an adult mussel.

Many estuarine bivalves have great commercial value. In New England, one of the most popular is the quahog (*Mercenaria mercenaria*), or hard-shell clam, seen in the lower color insert on page C-3. The name of this clam is derived from the Native American word for "wages" because at one time beads made from the shells *Mercenaria mercenaria* were used as currency. Growing from 2.75 to 4.25 inches (7 to 10.8 cm) long, these shellfish prefer low salinities. Quahogs have grayish yellow shells marked with clear rings, each of which represents a year's growth. Like oysters, quahogs are harvested commercially and by individuals.

Although both are bivalves, oysters and quahogs are easy to distinguish. Oyster shells are very rough and irregular. Oysters are sessile animals that grow in large colonies attached to substrates like rocks or piers. Unlike most other bivalves, the oyster lacks a foot and siphons, so must open its shell to circulate water over its gills. The common oyster (*Crassostrea virginica*), shown in the upper color insert on page C-4 is found along much of the eastern coast of North America.

Arthropods

Arthropods make up an extremely large group of animals in the estuary. Their terrestrial cousins are the familiar insects and spiders. Typical marine arthropods include crabs, shrimp, and barnacles, as well as the less conspicuous amphipods and copepods.

The body of an arthropod is covered with an *exoskeleton* that provides structural support and protection from predators. The tough skeletons of arthropods are primarily composed of *chitin*,

Advantages and Disadvantages of an Exoskeleton

More than 80 percent of the animal species are equipped with a hard, outer covering called an exoskeleton. The functions of exoskeletons are similar to those of other types of skeletal systems. Like the internal skeletons (endoskeletons) of amphibians, reptiles, birds, and mammals, exoskeletons support the tissues and give shape to the bodies of invertebrates. Exoskeletons offer some other advantages. Serving as a suit of armor, they are excellent protection against predators. Also, because they completely cover an animal's tissues, exoskeletons prevent them from drying out. In addition, exoskeletons serve as points of attachment for muscles, providing animals with more leverage and mechanical advantage than an endoskeleton can offer. That is why a tiny shrimp can cut a fish in half with its claw or lift an object 50 times heavier than its own body.

Despite all their good points, exoskeletons have some drawbacks. They are heavy, so the only animals that have been successful with them over time are those that have remained small. In addition, an animal must molt, or shed, its exoskeleton to grow. In Figure 4.2, a blue crab backs out of its old exoskeleton. During and immediately after a molt, an animal is unprotected and vulnerable to predators.

Fig. 4.2 A blue crab sheds its old shell so that it can grow; for a few days after, the crab is vulnerable to predators. (Courtesy Mary Hollinger, NODC biologist, NOAA)

an extremely hard, but highly flexible, polymer that is similar in structure to cellulose. Chitin is secreted by the animal's epidermis, the outermost layer of skin that lies just below the exoskeleton.

Arthropods' bodies are divided into segments. The head contains the brain, sensory organs, and structures that are specialized for taking in food. Some of the arthropod's sensory organs are compound eyes, which create multiple pictures and arrange them like tiles in a mosaic, and antennae, which interpret touch.

Arthropods, whose name translates to "joint-legged," are able to move quickly because they have *appendages* that are jointed. An appendage is a leg, antenna, or other part that extends from a segment of the body. Appendages are used for a variety of functions, including food handling, walking, swimming, and sensory input.

In most arthropods, males and females mate after ritualized courtships. In many species the male deposits sperm in the female's body, where they are held until eggs mature. As each egg leaves the ovary, stored sperm are released and fertilization occurs. Resulting zygotes mature into larvae that swim in the plankton for a short period of time before settling down on the reef floor to mature.

Crustaceans

Many of the arthropods are classified as crustaceans. The body segments of crustaceans are grouped into three specialized areas: head, thorax, and abdomen. The head is equipped with five pairs of appendages, two of which are antennae and three that are used for feeding. Some species of crustaceans have claws that are large and capable of exerting hundreds of pounds of pressure. The body and abdomen of a crustacean possesses walking or swimming appendages.

Two of the smallest types of estuarine crustaceans are the copepods and the amphipods. Both are important members of the zooplankton, where they serve as vital sources of food for larger animals. Copepods are extremely small, measuring less than 0.04 inch (1 mm) in length. Their white or transparent torpedo-shaped bodies have forked tails. On the anterior end, a copepod possesses two antennae that are as long as its body.

Copepods feed on single-celled algae and other small organisms in the plankton. To stay afloat, many of their appendages are modified with hairlike extensions that increase surface area and slow their sinking rate. In addition, their tiny bodies contain globules of oil, which are less dense than water and float on top of it. Copepods swim by backward strokes of their long antennae and trunk appendages, a technique that moves their bodies forward with jerky motions.

Fertilization in copepods is internal. Fertilized eggs are carried in a special structure called the ovisac that is located under segments on the female's abdomen. The hatchlings, which are called nauplius larvae, float and swim weakly in the water column as they mature into adult forms.

Amphipods are shrimplike crustaceans that may be found in the water column or in the substrate. Slightly larger than copepods, these crustaceans are omnivores that feed on plant matter, diatoms, and animal material. Unlike copepods, the larvae of amphipods do not swim in the plankton. Females carry fertilized eggs in a brood pouch where the young animals remain after hatching. As they mature, they swim from the pouch to begin life as adultlike young animals.

Barnacles are sessile crustaceans that live within enclosures made of calcified plates. Each animal spends its life attached to wood, rock, or some other solid surface, positioned so that its heads is down and legs are sticking out into the water. When exposed to air during low tide, a barnacle closes its plates to prevent drying. Small openings between plates allow moist air to circulate over the gills, providing oxygen.

Barnacles are hermaphrodites, but individuals usually cross-fertilize. One barnacle transfers sperm to a neighbor through a long tube that it extends between them. Fertilized eggs develop into zygotes that later form larvae. After a time of swimming in the plankton, larvae settle on a substrate, exude a brown, glue-like material that anchors them in place, and metamorphose into adult forms.

Acorn barnacles, named for their acorn shapes, are found on hard estuarine substrates like rocks, shells, or the pilings of docks and piers. A widespread acorn barnacle in British estuaries is the Northern rock barnacle (*Semibalanus balanoides*). The adults are shrimplike animals covered by overlapping, protective plates. When underwater, the plates open and six pair of feathery, handlike appendages called cirri extend to collect bits of food floating in the water. Barnacles can only feed when they are immersed in water, so those that are uncovered during low tide cannot feed as often, or grow as quickly, as fully immersed animals.

Fig. 4.3   White shrimp, one of several edible species, depend on estuaries for their survival. (Courtesy of National Estuarine Research Reserve Collection, NOAA)

Shrimp, lobsters, and crabs are estuarine crustaceans that are closely related to each other. Each has five pairs of legs, the first of which is often modified as a claw. Shrimp are small, 10-legged animals that have relatively lightweight exoskeletons and gills located under their shells. Unlike lobsters and crabs, shrimp are primarily swimmers instead of crawlers, propelling their bodies through the water with long, muscular tails. Their eyes, supported on stalks, keep watch for predators.

White shrimp (*Penaeus setiferus*), shown in Figure 4.3, and the closely related brown shrimp and pink shrimp spend portions of their lives in estuaries. The white shrimp is large, reaching 10 inches (25 cm) in length, with brown antennae that are longer than its body. Three of the five pairs of walking legs end in weak pincers. Brown shrimp have dark green and red uropods, appendages that make up the tail fan, while those of pink shrimp have a bluish color. Shrimp use their different kinds of appendages for locomotion. Walking legs carry the animal short distances across substrates. Swimming legs are adapted for long-distance traveling. The uropod can be flipped to quickly propel the animal backward and out of harm's way.

Habitats for white shrimp include the muddy floors of estuaries and salt marshes. During spawning, an offshore event, the male transfers packets of sperm to the female, which she attaches to her underside. Later, when she broadcasts eggs into the water, they are fertilized externally by the stored sperm. Fertilized eggs settle to the seafloor for one or two days before hatching into planktonic larvae called nauplii that mature through several larval stages, each a little larger than the last. Young shrimp in the post-larval stage, a period when they look like miniature adults, return to the estuary to feed and mature. They migrate toward the freshwater inflow because that is the region where food is most abundant. Young shrimp feed on plants and organic matter, but as they mature they begin preying on animals such as worms, larvae of fish and shellfish, and even other shrimp. The following spring, the mature shrimp move out of the estuary and back into the ocean for breeding season.

Blue mud shrimp (*Upogebia pugettensis*) are most often found on the muddy bottoms of estuaries and salt marshes. A male and female pair of blue mud shrimp dig a roomy burrow, which may extend downward for 17.7 inches (45 cm), level off with a horizontal tunnel about 39.4 inches long (100 cm), then angle back up toward the surface. The shrimp remove mud from their burrow in a basket that they form with their first two pairs of "hairy" thoracic legs. These six-inch (15.2-cm) long crustaceans also use their legs to strain food particles from water. Like white shrimp, a female mud shrimp broods her young on her abdomen. From time to time she aerates the eggs by circulating water over them with her swimming appendages.

Several groups of animals are described as crabs. Like all crustaceans, crabs have hard, protective exoskeletons. Their bodies are flattened, an adaptation for squeezing into small spaces. Compared to shrimp and lobsters, the abdomens of crabs are small, and are designed to fit up close to their bodies.

Depending on the species, crabs display a variety of feeding strategies. The sizes and shapes of their claws reveal the food preferences of each species. For example, those with spoon-shaped claws feed on algae, which they scoop up or scrape off rocks. Shellfish-eating crabs have big claws with dull, broad teeth that can break open exoskeletons and shells. Claws of scavengers are sharp, enabling them to tear apart dead plants and animals. Filter-feeding species have claws that scoop up mud from which they isolate organic material.

The true crabs, as shown in Figure 4.4, have five pairs of walking legs, one of which is modified as claws. Although they can crawl forward slowly, crabs usually run sideways with a skittering motion. During mating season, crabs display extensive mating rituals. Males dig burrows, then attract females to them by waving their claws and rapping on the burrows. Once a female has chosen a mate with an appropriate home, she enters the burrow and stays in it until she lays her eggs.

Fig. 4.4   Crabs have five pairs of walking legs, one of which is modified as claws.

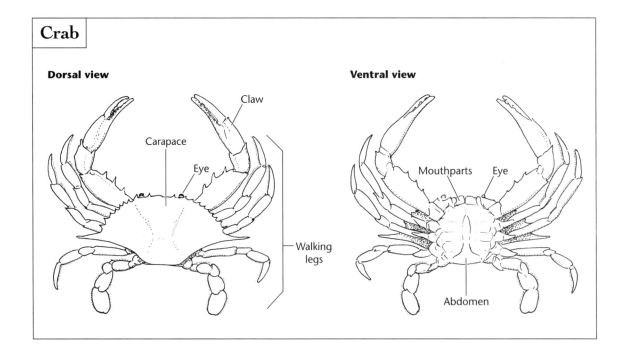

Crab

Dorsal view

Claw

Carapace

Eye

Walking legs

Ventral view

Mouthparts   Eye

Abdomen

Estuaries are home to several types of crabs, including blue, Dungeness, sand, stone, green, fiddler and snow crabs. Blue crabs (*Callinectes*), which are brown or olive green dorsally with blue claws and legs, are usually six to nine inches (15.2 to 22.8 cm) wide. They have a set of pincers along with three sets of walking legs, and a pair that is modified for swimming. Stalked eyes help them see all around, including behind.

A male blue crab has a T-shaped abdomen, while the female has a rounded one. Before her final molt, an immature female, or "she-crab," may be protected by a male, who carries her under his body. Just after the female molts and while her shell is soft, she unfolds her abdomen so that the male can transfer sperm to it. The male continues his protection of the female until her new shell hardens. Females can store viable sperm in their bodies up to a year. Later in the season, the female produces eggs, which are fertilized as they travel over the stored sperm. Blue crabs usually produce 1.75 to 2 million eggs with each spawn and may spawn twice in a season, using the same store of sperm on each occasion. The eggs are laid in a spongy mass that the female attaches to her body. Hatchlings are tiny larvae that go through a succession of molts and seven larval stages. Adults spend their entire lives in the estuarine waters, feeding on a variety of items, including bivalves, other crabs, crustaceans, plants, and dead organisms.

Fiddler crabs are some of the most common types seen in salt marshes and tidal flats. Easily distinguished from other crabs by their small, square bodies and single oversize claws, fiddlers forage for food along the banks when the tide is out. To feed, they scoop up mud in their claws and eat the decaying organic matter in it.

Only the males have one large and one small claw; females have two small ones. A male waves his enlarged claw to attract the attention of a female or to scare away a potential predator. During spring tides, a male prepares a burrow where a female will rest for two weeks while her developing eggs incubate. When she emerges from the burrow, she releases the eggs, which are swept out to sea on the tide. For two weeks hatchlings drift and develop in the ocean, then return to the estuary banks on the next spring tide. Before the tiny hatchlings reach the adult form, they go through five different stages of development. Most fiddler crabs live one to one and a half years.

Fiddler crab burrows can be complex, with more than one entrance. The half-inch (1.2-cm) wide doorways lead to tunnels that reach depths of 1 foot (30 cm). Atlantic marsh fiddler crabs (*Uca pugnax*) always stay close to their burrows, jumping into their own, or their neighbor's, when frightened. Burrows are cool and provide places for the crabs to rest out of the heat of the Sun. During high tide, burrow openings can be plugged with balls of mud to keep out water. Even if water covers the burrows, air trapped in the tunnels enables crabs

Mud Lobster

In mangrove estuaries, the mud lobster plays a special role in supporting the growth and health of mangrove trees. The mud lobster (*Thalassina anomala*) is not a true lobster but rather a crustacean that is more closely related to crabs. Shy by nature, a mud lobster digs around mangrove roots, excavating tunnels that may be 2.2 yards (2 m) deep and creating volcano-shaped piles of dirt that are 3.3 yards (3 m) tall. During the day, the mud lobster stays inside its U-shaped burrow, but at night it emerges and continues digging.

Mud lobsters dig to find detritus, their favorite food. To meet their nutritional needs, a lobster must process a tremendous amount of soil, so digging is a constant chore. The constant excavation benefits the mangrove estuary ecosystem in several ways. Nutrients that were buried in deep layers of mud are brought closer to the surface, within the reach of plant roots. Digging also makes it possible for oxygen, and oxygenated water, to find its way into layers of the soil that would normally be oxygen-depleted. Newly dug soil provides an ideal environment for mangrove seedlings; those that fall into the mud lobster's dredging grow faster than those that fall in other locations.

A mud lobster mound provides homes for other animals in the mangrove estuary. Because the mound is tall, it is not as wet as the soil around it. Ants, spiders, clams, snakes, and worms that cannot survive in soggy soil move into the mound. Several species of plants, including the sea holly (*Acanthus*) and blind-your-eye (*Exoecaria algallocha*), find the mounds to be ideal habitats. The presence of mud lobster mounds increases species diversity in the area.

to breath. Like crabs that live underwater, fiddler and other land-based crabs have gills, but they use them to breathe air. To do so, their gills must stay moist. For this reason, Atlantic marsh fiddler crabs and other species can never stray very far from the water.

Hermit crabs are distinguished from true crabs by their two pairs of walking legs. Because a hermit crab lacks a hard exoskeleton over its abdomen, it moves into an abandoned snail shell to protect its soft body. To fit into the shell, the crab backs its twisted abdomen into the curved interior space, holding its body in place with two sets of hind legs that are adapted as grippers. If threatened, the crab can fully retreat into the shell and block the opening with its claws. As hermit crabs grow, they must abandon their old homes and find larger shells that can accommodate their expanding sizes.

In the estuary, the long-clawed hermit crab (*Pagurus longicarpus*) prefers the shells of periwinkles and oyster drills. A relatively small animal, the long-clawed hermit crab only grows to a maximum length of two inches (5 cm). The flat-clawed hermit crab (*Pagurus arcuatus*) is larger and lives in shells of moon snails and whelks.

Horseshoe Crabs

Horseshoe crabs are more closely related to spiders than to crabs. The horseshoe-shaped shell ends in a long tail that serves as rudders as the animal swims. On the dorsal side of the shell are two compound eyes and two simple eyes. Underneath the shell are five pairs of legs, the first four modified for walking and the last pair for swimming. The gills, which resemble the folded pages of a book, are located near the posterior end. Horseshoe crabs feed on burrowing mollusks and worms.

On the eastern coast of the United States, millions of Atlantic horseshoe crabs (*Limulus polyphemus*) crawl ashore in bays and estuaries from Maine to the Gulf of Mexico to mate. Mating occurs on the night of a full moon after spring tides in late spring. The spring tides make it possible for the crabs to deposit their eggs high up on the shores. During mating, the smaller male hangs onto the female's back, attaching himself with special hooks located on his first pair of legs. The female digs a hole and deposits her eggs, which are immediately fertilized by the male. Four weeks later, the hatchlings, half-inch (1.2-cm) larvae that look like miniature adults enter the shallow estuarine waters where they spend their youth, molting their exoskeletons several times as they grow.

Echinoderms

Sea stars (starfish), sea cucumbers, and sea urchins are echinoderms, or spiny-skinned animals. All echinoderms are radially symmetrical, and most have five or more body sections extending from a central disc. The bodies of echinoderms are supported by internal skeletons, solid in some species and jointed in others. Because their mouths are located on the ventral surface, they are close to the substrate. An echinoderm's anus is located on the ventral side. As a group, echinoderms show a variety of nutritional strategies and, depending on the species, may be carnivores, detritivores, or herbivores.

Tentacle-like structures called tube feet, shown in Figure 4.5, are used for locomotion and for grasping prey. The tube feet act like suction pads, clutching and releasing surfaces as the animals move across them. The suction pads are operated by a system that supplies water through small tubes to individual suction cups. As the tube feet press against an object, water is withdrawn, creating suction. When water is returned to the cups, the suction is broken, and the tube feet release their grip.

In echinoderms, sexes are separate and fertilization is external. Zygotes develop into larvae, which swim in the plankton for a short time, then settle to the bottom and take on typical echinoderm features. Most echinoderms can also reproduce asexually. If part of the animal breaks off, it may grow into a complete, new organism. All species are capable of regenerating lost body parts such as limbs, spines, and in some cases, intestines.

The common sea star (*Asterias forbesi*) is a red or orange animal that grows to about 5.1 inches (13 cm) in width. Like

other sea stars, this voracious predator feeds on bivalves by separating their shells with its strong legs. As the shells part, the sea star's stomach pushes the opening between the shells. Digestive juices in the echinoderm's stomach dissolve the mussel tissue, which the stomach then absorbs. When the meal is over, the sea star retracts its stomach and crawls to another mussel.

Sea urchins are echinoderms that look like balls of spines. Their bodies are protected and supported internally by 10 sections of rigid shell that extend from the ventral mouth to the dorsal anus, like sections of an orange. The mouth contains a feeding structure called Aristotle's lantern, a beak-like instrument made of five teeth that are designed to scrape algae from rocks. The purple sea urchin (*Arbacia punctulata*) is a four-inch (10.2-cm) echinoderm whose body is covered in

Fig. 4.5   On its ventral side, a sea star (starfish) has a centrally located mouth and tube feet on each of its radiating arms. (Courtesy of Dr. James P. McVey, NOAA Sea Grant Program)

one-inch (2.5-cm) tapering purple spines. Tube feet enable the purple sea urchin to move slowly across the substrate.

A sea cucumber is a tubular animal that resembles a fat worm. Instead of lying on its mouth like other spiny-skinned animals, a sea cucumber lies on its side, with its mouth at one end of the tube and anus at the other end. Around the mouth, several tube feet are modified to form tentacles. Some species use their tentacles to catch bits of food suspended in water or pick up sediment that contains food. The respiratory structures of these animals are located alongside the digestive tract.

Sea cucumbers have an effective, although unusual, defense tactic called auto evisceration. If threatened, a sea cucumber sprays its intestines, either through its mouth or a break in its body wall, on its intruder. The sticky digestive material deters most predators. The lost and damaged body parts are able to regenerate within a few days.

In the estuary, *Labidoplax media* is a sea cucumber that lives atop muddy and sandy bottoms or just beneath the sediment. *Labidoplax media* is small, measuring only 0.8 to 1.6 inches (2 to 4 cm) in length and its transparent, wormlike body lacks tube feet. Twelve tentacles, all about the same size, surround the mouth.

Cucumaria frondosa, another species of sea cucumber, has a brown or dark blue body and tough skin. The 10 tentacles around its mouth are colorful and bushy. Growing to lengths of 19.7 inches (50 cm), this large sea cucumber has five double rows of tube feet. *Cucumaria frondosa* prefers rocky substrates over muddy ones.

Conclusion

Mollusks, crustaceans, and echinoderms are well represented in the estuary. The food-rich, shallow-water environment provided by bay waters suit numerous species of all three groups. Some types spend their entire lives in the estuary, while others use it for a nursery where their young grow and develop in relative safety from predators.

Mollusks such as bivalves and gastropods make their homes in the intertidal regions of estuaries. Bivalves are soft-bodied animals that are protected by two strong shells. Their bodies are covered by a mantle, a sheet of tissue that excretes the shell and some defensive chemicals. Most are filter feeders that trap small bits of food in the mucus on their gills. Clams, mussels, and oysters are examples of coastal bivalves.

Gastropods, soft-bodied animals that live in one shell or completely lack a shell, are abundant throughout the estuary system. Estuarine gastropods include a number of snails such as moon snails, black turbans, and oyster drills. Gastropods are generally predators that feed on bivalves by climbing atop their shells and secreting juices that weaken them, making it possible for the predators to drill holes in the shells with their sharp radulae. Once a hole is created, the gastropods flood the victims' soft bodies with digestive enzymes, then suck out the soupy mixture.

Crustaceans are invertebrates whose segmented bodies are protected with tough exoskeletons. In the estuary, crustaceans include bug-like amphipods and isopods, shrimp, and crabs. All of these animals are equipped with appendages for walking, swimming, or both. In most, fertilization is internal and fertilized eggs are brooded on legs or swimmerets. Close relatives to the crustaceans are the horseshoe crabs, animals that share some characteristics with terrestrial spiders.

Echinoderms are known as spiny-skinned animals because their protective outer layer is tough and prickly. The bodies of these animals are radial, and most are divided into five equal parts. Sea stars, brittle stars, sea urchins, sand dollars, and sea cucumbers are examples of this large group. They are all capable of slow movement on their hydraulically controlled tube feet. Sea stars prey on bivalves, using their tiny tube feet to pull apart the bivalves' shells. Once open, sea stars push their stomachs onto the bodies of their victims, then digest and absorb the bivalves before pulling their stomachs back inside. Echinoderms also have incredible powers of regeneration, enabling them to replace a lost leg or torn section of intestine.

 # Fish
Growing Up in the Ocean's Nursery

*E*stuaries are one of the few environments capable of supporting both saltwater and freshwater fish. Worldwide, fish make up the largest group of vertebrates. Some estuarine fish species spend the majority of their lives in these environments of mixed fresh and salt water. Others are part-time residents, either visiting estuaries during spawning or living there as juveniles.

Compared to most marine environments, estuaries contain a disproportionately large number of young fish. Many oceanic species breed offshore, and their young travel to the estuary where they can hide from predators among its many nooks and crannies. This haven is well stocked with food to sustain the young fish until they are large enough to return safely to join the adults in the open sea.

There are two major groups of fish: cartilaginous fish and bony fish. The former includes rays and sharks, and only a few species of either can be found in estuaries. In the latter group are hundreds of bony fish that spend some or all of their time there.

Cartilaginous Fish

Worldwide, estuaries are homes to several species of stingrays. The Atlantic stingray (*Dasyatis sabina*) is a typical representative of the group. A seasonal migrant, the Atlantic stingray is found in shallow estuarine water of the Atlantic coastline during summer and fall. When temperatures get cold, it moves to warmer, deeper waters off the coast. Measuring only one foot (30 cm) across its disk, this small fish is brown on the topside and white underneath. The snout is triangular, the edges of the outer disks rounded, and the pectoral fins fused with the head. Near the base of the tail, a hard spine or barb contains venom-secreting cells.

The Atlantic stingray favors water that is less than three feet (0.9 m) deep. When feeding, the animal swims very close to the sandy bottom of the estuary so that it can search for food in the sediment. The ray makes frequent stops, lying motionless on the sand and evaluating the soil underneath for prey. Because its eyes are on the top of its head, the stingray detects prey hidden in the soil by sensing the natural electric fields they produce. If prey is found, the ray waves its pelvic fins up and down, an action that creates a small depression in the sand and uncovers the victim. The diet of the Atlantic stingray consists of bottom-dwelling, or benthic, invertebrates such as anemones, worms, amphipods, isopods, bivalves, and brittle stars.

Teeth of the Atlantic stingray have flat, blunt surfaces that are ideal for crushing shells and hard exoskeletons. During mating season, teeth in the males take on a long, narrow shape, curving toward the corners of the mouth. Mating season begins in the fall and continues through the spring, although ovulation does not occur until early spring. During courtship, the male swims closely behind the female, nipping at her body and fins. To insert sperm internally, the male holds the female by gripping her pectoral fins with his long cusps. The resulting embryos develop within the female's body over a period of almost four months. During the first three-quarters of embryonic life, the developing stingrays are nourished by yolk from their eggs. After that, they receive uterine milk that is produced by the mother. Three or four tiny offspring, measuring only about seven inches (10 cm), are born in late summer.

Several species of sharks can be found in estuaries. Member of the family Carcharhinidae, the requiem sharks, are well represented. As a rule, requiem sharks are voracious predators that feed on fish, bottom-dwelling invertebrates, turtles, and seabirds. More active at night than in the day, they can be found swimming alone or in small groups. Depending on the species, Carcharhinidae may be ovoviviparous or viviparous.

Shark Anatomy

Although there are many kinds of sharks, they all are similar anatomically. A shark's digestive system begins at the mouth, which is filled with teeth. Shark teeth are continuously produced, and at any time a shark may have 3,000 teeth arranged in six to 20 rows. As older teeth are lost from the front rows, younger ones move forward and replace them. Teeth are adapted to specific kinds of food. Depending on their species, sharks may have thin, daggerlike teeth for holding prey; serrated, wedge-shaped teeth for cutting and tearing; or small, conical teeth that can crush animals in shells.

The internal skeletons of sharks are made of cartilage, a lightweight and flexible bonelike material. Their external surfaces are very tough and rugged. Sharks have extremely flexible skin that is covered with placoid scales, each of which is pointed and has a rough edge on it. Shark fins are rigid and cannot be folded down like the fins of bony fish.

Like other aquatic organisms, sharks get the oxygen they need to live from the water. Compared to air, water contains a small percentage of dissolved oxygen. Surface waters may contain five milliliters of oxygen per liter of water, dramatically less than the 210 ml of oxygen per liter of air that is available to land animals. To survive, fish must be very efficient at removing and concentrating the oxygen in water.

In aquatic organisms, gills carry out the function of lungs in terrestrial animals. To respire, sharks pull water in through their mouths and *spiracles,* holes on top of their

A typical estuarine requiem shark is the sandbar shark (*Carcharhinus plumbeus*) which, as its name suggests, favors sandbars as well as sandy and muddy bottoms. Found in tropic and temperate waters worldwide, the sandbar shark has a tall, triangular-shaped dorsal fin and a rounded short snout. This stoutly built shark is brown or dark blue dorsally, white or pale on the ventral surface, and intermediate shades on the sides. Adult females may be eight feet (2.4 m) long, but males are somewhat shorter, averaging about six feet (1.6 m). Viviparous females reproduce once every two years, yielding eight to 10 young after a gestation period of 12 months. Sandbar sharks mature slowly, reaching reproductive age between three and 13 years. Because their life spans are only 21 years, these sharks have a relatively short number

heads. The water passes over their gills and exits through the gill slits on the sides of the head. Most species of sharks can pump water over their gills by opening and closing their mouths. Some sharks, the "ram ventilators," must swim continuously to move water over their gills. Oxygen in water is picked up by tiny blood vessels in the gills, then carried to the heart, a small two-chambered, S-shaped tube. From there, oxygenated blood is pumped to the rest of the body.

Sharks fertilize their eggs internally. Males transfer sperm to females using modified pelvic fins. Some species are *oviparous,* which means the female lays fertilized eggs. Shark eggs may be deposited in lagoons or shallow reef water, where they incubate for six to 15 months. Many of the eggs' cases are equipped with hairy or leathery tendrils that help hold them to rocks or plants. Other species are *viviparous,* so the embryos develop inside the mother and are born alive. Several species are *ovoviviparous,* which means that the embryo develops inside an egg within the female's body. The egg hatches inside the mother, the hatchling eats the yolk and any unfertilized eggs, then is born alive.

Shark populations are relatively small compared to other kinds of fish. One reason is because shark reproduction rates are low. Unlike fish and many of the invertebrates, a female shark produces only a few offspring each year. In addition, the gestation period, time when the embryo develops inside the mother, of viviparous species is long.

of reproductive years, a factor that causes their populations to remain small.

Another shark that spends a lot of time in estuaries around the world is the hammerhead shark (*Sphyrna zygaena*), shown in Figure 5.1. Light gray to dark gray dorsally and white ventrally, this large shark grows to 11.5 feet (3.5 m) in length and can weigh more than 500 pounds (230 kg), although specimens have been found that weigh 1,000 pounds (450 kg). The hammerhead's thick, rectangular-shaped head makes it easy to identify. The first dorsal fin is tall and erect, just the type that is often associated with sharks. The hammerhead migrates north in summer, visiting estuaries and other nearshore environments, where it feeds on small sharks, skates, rays, fish, crustaceans, bivalves, and cephalopods.

Fig. 5.1   The rectangular heads of hammerhead sharks make them easy to recognize. (Courtesy of Getty Images)

The leopard shark (*Galeocerdo cuvier*), a strong swimmer that often travels in groups, is a midsize shark that grows to 51.1 inches (130 cm). Very common in estuaries and lagoons, leopard sharks are most often found in sandy or muddy areas where they swim close to the bottom and feed on crustaceans, bivalves, and worms. Their snouts are broad and short, and their dorsal fins are rounded instead of triangular like some other species of sharks. On the dorsal side, the body is gray to bronze, with large dark saddles and dots that fade laterally and blend into a lighter ventral surface. Leopard sharks produce four to 29 live pups per litter.

Bony Fish

The majority of fish have bony skeletons, and their diversity is astounding. Some fish are shaped like torpedoes but others are as flat as pancakes. Many tropical species are brightly colored and marked with vivid lines and spots, while most of the temperate and cold-water types are more subtly pigmented. Some types of fish undertake long, arduous migratory trips and others spend their entire lives in one small area.

Estuaries are stopovers for several species of migratory bony fish, both catadromous and anadromous types. Catadromous fish, such as the American eel, live in or near freshwater during most of their lives, but travel to the ocean to spawn. Anadromous fish, like the American shad, travel from saline to freshwater to breed.

Other kinds of fish that do not fall into these two reproductive classifications also rely on the estuaries for food as well as spawning and nursery grounds. The dover sole, starry flounder, and hundreds of other species spawn in the open sea and send their young to the estuary to mature. Herring and chum are examples of species that spawn in or near the estuaries. Their hatchlings grow to fingerlings in the estuarine nurseries before they move to open sea.

Anadromous fish in the estuarine system greatly outnumber the catadromous species. One of the best-known anadromous types is the salmon. The term *salmon* is used to describe several species in the family Salmonidae, a group of fish whose long bodies are covered with rounded scales. A typical salmon has a spotted back and a fleshy fin between the dorsal fin and tail. Various species, all with complex life cycles, make their homes in the North Pacific on the North American and Asiatic coasts as well as in the North Atlantic on the North American and European coasts. The events in a salmon's life cycle are detailed in Figure 5.3.

In the spring, Atlantic salmon (*Salmo salar*) eggs hatch from nests called redds that are located in freshwater streams. Hatchlings, or alevins, live on the nourishment of the yolk sacs. After six weeks, the yolk sacs are completely absorbed, and the alevins are called fry. Fry emerge from the nests to look for insect larvae and other small prey in the streambed. As they feed and grow, fry develop into parr, a stage in which their two-inch (5-cm) bodies are camouflaged with vertical stripes, a coloration that protects them from their predators as they forage for food. Parr live in the streams of their birth for

Bony Fish Anatomy

All bony fish share many physical characteristics, which are labeled in Figure 5.2. One of their distinguishing features is scaly skin. Scales on fish overlap one another, much like shingles on a roof, protecting the skin from damage and slowing the movement of water into or out of the fish's body.

Bony fish are outfitted with fins that facilitate maneuvering and positioning in the water. The fins, which are made of thin membranes supported by stiff pieces of cartilage, can be folded down or held upright. Fins are named for their location: Dorsal fins are on the back, a caudal fin is at the tail, and an anal fin is on the ventral side. Two sets of lateral fins are located on the sides of the fish, the pectoral fins are toward the head, and the pelvic fins are near the tail. The caudal fin moves the fish forward in the water, and the others help change direction and maintain balance.

Although fish dine on a wide assortment of food, most species are predators whose mouths contain small teeth for grasping prey. Nutrients from digested food are distributed through the body by a system of closed blood vessels. The circulation of blood is powered by a muscular two-chambered heart. Blood entering the heart is depleted of oxygen and filled with carbon dioxide, a waste product of metabolism. Blood collects in the upper chamber, the atrium, before it is pushed into the ventricle. From the ventricle, it travels to the gills where it picks up oxygen and gets rid of its carbon dioxide. Water exits through a single gill slit on the side of the head. The gill slits of fish are covered with a protective flap, the operculum.

In many bony fish, some gases in the blood are channeled into another organ, the swim bladder. This organ is essentially a gas bag that helps the fish control its depth by adjusting its buoyancy. A fish can float higher in the water by increasing the volume of gas in the swim bladder. To sink, the fish reduces the amount of gas in the bladder.

Most bony fish reproduce externally. Females lay hundreds of eggs in the water, then males swim by and release milt, a fluid containing sperm, on the eggs. Fertilization occurs in the open water, and the parents swim away, leaving the eggs unprotected. Not all of the eggs are fertilized, and many that are fertilized will become victims of predators, so only a small percentage of eggs hatch.

Fig. 5.2 *The special features of bony fish include bony scales (a), opercula (b), highly maneuverable fins (c), a tail with its upper and lower lobes usually of equal size (d), a swim bladder that adjusts the fish's buoyancy (e), nostrils (f), pectoral fins (g), a pelvic fin (h), an anal fin (i), lateral lines (j), dorsal fins (k), and a stomach (l).*

Features of Bony Fish

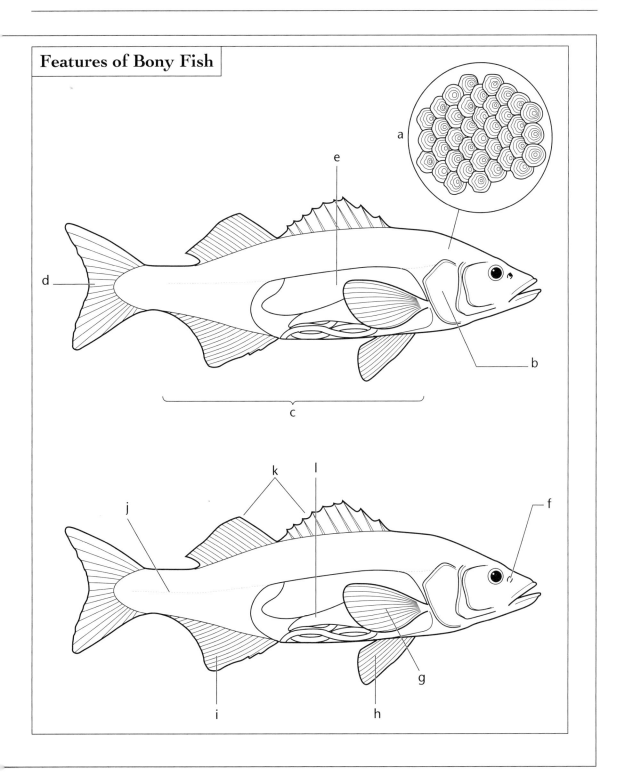

Life Cycle of a Salmon

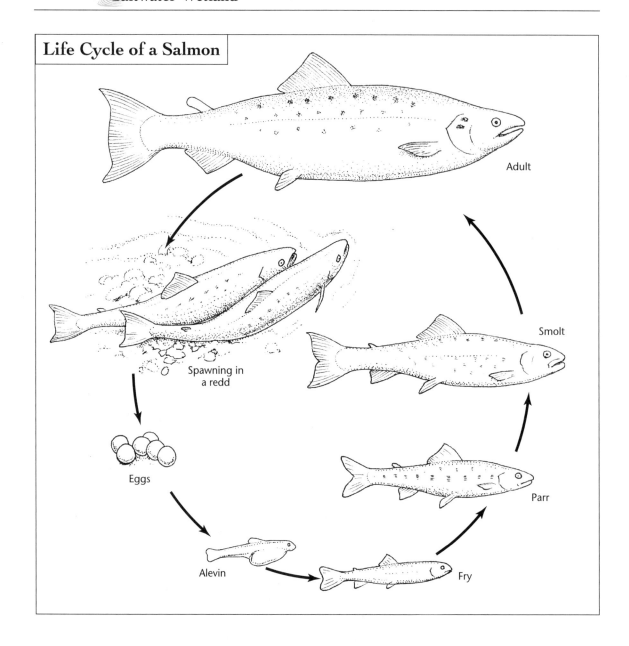

Adult

Smolt

Spawning in
a redd

Parr

Eggs

Alevin   Fry

Fig. 5.3 Salmon live in freshwater, estuaries, and salt water at different stages in their lives.

the next one to three years. At the end of this period, they are known as smolts.

Six-inch (15.2-cm) long, silver-colored smolts undergo a change in body chemistry that enables them to live in salt water. Before moving from the stream to the sea, smolts spend some time in the brackish estuarine waters, giving their bodies

▲ *The Ashe Island Estuary, south of Charleston, South Carolina*
(Courtesy of National Estuarine Research Reserve Collection, NOAA)

▲ *Cord grass is a major producer in the saltwater wetlands that surround temperate estuaries.* (Courtesy of National Estuarine Research Reserve Collection, NOAA)

▲ *The red and green anemone* (Telia crassicornis) *lives in shallow estuarine waters.* (Courtesy of National Estuarine Research Reserve Collection, NOAA)

▲ *An upside-down jellyfish* (Cassiopeia xamachana) *is common in estuaries with soft-sediment bottoms.* (Courtesy of National Estuarine Research Reserve Collection, NOAA)

▲ *Marsh periwinkles* (Littorina irrorata) *climb stalks of grass in saltwater wetlands.* (Courtesy of Mary Hollinger, NODC biologist, NOAA)

▲ *The Northern quahog* (Mercenaria mercenaria) *is a bivalve that favors substrates made of a mixture of mud and sand.* (Courtesy of National Estuarine Research Reserve Collection, NOAA)

▲ *Oysters, like this* Crassostrea virginica, *attach to substrates in estuaries.* (Courtesy of National Estuarine Research Reserve Collection, NOAA)

▲ *The Atlantic sturgeon* (Acipenser oxyrhynchus) *feeds on prey that it digs up from the bottom of the estuary.* (Courtesy of U.S. Fish and Wildlife Service)

▲ *The American eel* (Anguilla rostrata) *is born in or near freshwater, then travels to the ocean to breed.* (Courtesy of U.S. Fish and Wildlife Service)

▲ *Diamondback turtles lay their eggs in shallow nests on sandy beaches.* (Courtesy of The Coastline Collection, NOAA)

▲ *The loggerhead sea turtle* (Caretta caretta) *is named for its large head.* (Courtesy of National Estuarine Research Reserve Collection, NOAA)

▲ *The great egret* (Casmerodius albus) *feeds and nests near the estuary.* (Courtesy of U.S. Fish and Wildlife Service)

▲ *Brown pelicans* (Pelecanus occidentalis) *dive into the water and scoop up fish with their expandable bills.* (Courtesy of U.S. Fish and Wildlife Service)

▲ *Black skimmers* (Rynchops niger) *have jutting lower jaws that they skim through the water to pick up prey.* (Courtesy of U.S. Fish and Wildlife Service)

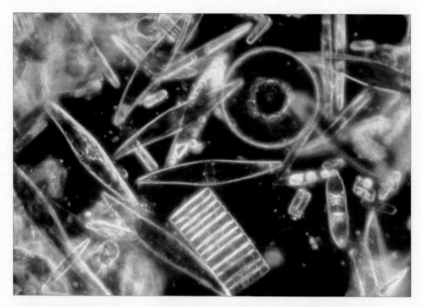

▲ *Diatoms, microscopic organisms that have a variety of shapes, are key producers in saltwater wetlands.* (Courtesy of Dr. Neil Sullivan, University of Southern California, NOAA)

▲ *Diamondback turtles* (Malachlenys terrapin), *like this adult female, are only found in estuaries.* (Courtesy of Mary Hollinger, NODC biologist, NOAA)

time to adjust to the changes in salinity. Smolts live in the ocean for the next two to four years, during which time they grow into adult fish that weigh from eight to 15 pounds (3.6 to 6.8 kg).

When it is time to breed, adult salmon begin a trip back to the freshwater streams where they were born. Traveling as much as 70 miles (115 km) a day, adults locate their natal streams using their remarkable memories and keen senses of smell. Each birth stream has a unique odor, a chemical signature, which results from the particular combination of its plants, animals, minerals, and soils. On the way back to their natal streams, salmon spend time in estuaries, resting and adjusting to changes in salinity. Once they enter freshwater, the salmon do not feed again until they return to the ocean.

The female of a mating pair selects the spawning site and digs a nest by waving her body to and fro, clearing an area that may be as large as 10 feet (3 m) long and 12 inches (30 cm) deep. Male and female lie side by side, shedding eggs and sperm. After the eggs are fertilized, the female buries them. Spawning is repeated several times over the next month, each event requiring a new nest (redd). When spawning is over, the tired, starving adults, which are called kelts, begin to slowly drift back downstream to the estuary and eventually back to the ocean. Fish that are too weak for the journey back to sea may spend the winter in the creek or die attempting the return trip.

Atlantic menhaden (*Brevoortia tyrannus*) are schooling fish that live in estuarine waters along the Atlantic coast from Nova Scotia to Florida. Some make their way as far north as the Chesapeake during the summer but migrate to southern waters in fall and winter. During the spring, Atlantic menhaden spawn offshore, producing larvae that swim into estuaries to feed on phytoplankton and zooplankton. By fall, having reached lengths of seven inches (17.8 cm), they migrate south with the adult fish. If young Atlantic menhaden escape predation by birds and large fish, they eventually grow to 15 inches (38 cm) in length. Some are parasitized by a crustacean that attaches to their mouths, giving Atlantic menhaden the nickname of "bugfish."

The Atlantic sturgeon (*Acipenser oxyrhynchus*) is a primitive type of fish that dates back 70 million years. As shown in the lower color insert on page C-4, its body is covered with rows of bony plates called scutes instead of scales. The Atlantic sturgeon can usually be found on the bottom of the estuary, where it roots up prey, especially crustaceans and mollusks, with its snout.

Like many other anadromous fish, during the spring Atlantic sturgeons travel through estuaries on their way to freshwater spawning sites. Their hatchlings rely on the resources in estuaries during a period of feeding and growth. Reproductive rates in sturgeons are low because each adult fish only spawns every two to six years. During a spawning season, each female releases about 800,000 to 3.7 million large, sticky eggs that scatter in the water and eventually attach to the sea floor. Females reach reproductive age in 12 years, but the males mature faster. Sturgeons are long-lived fish that can survive up to 60 years.

The smaller and shorter-lived American shad (*Alosa sapidissima*) is another anadromous species. In the spring, adults swim to the estuary and upstream into its rivers, traveling for days without eating. The offspring move downstream to the estuary, where they feed and grow. After spawning, the adults return to sea where most of them die. Striped bass (*Morone saxatilis*), or rockfish have breeding strategies similar to those of American shad. The elongated bodies of striped bass have about seven blue-green stripes dorsally and are silver-colored on the undersides. Males may reach lengths of 45 inches (114.3 cm) and females 72 inches (182.8 cm).

The American eel (*Anguilla rostrata*), shown in the upper color insert on page C-5, is one of the few catadromous estuarine fish species. The life cycle of an American eel begins life as a 2-inch (5-cm) larva floating amid plankton in the Sargasso Sea, north of the Bahamas. After about a year, the young eel moves to coastal waters and metamorphoses into the stage called a transparent glass eel. During the fall, the glass eel migrates into an estuary to feed and, while there, its body takes on color. Once fully pigmented with yellow-green on the dorsal side and whitish gray on the ventral, the young eel is known as an elver. An elver remains in fresh or brackish water in this yellow phase for most of its life, a period that varies from five to 20 years. Females grow to a maximum length of five feet (1.5 m); males are somewhat smaller.

When it is time for an adult eel to spawn, it undergoes several dramatic physical and behavioral changes. Feeding stops completely, and the eyes and pectoral fins enlarge. Pigments in the eel's skin change to gray on the dorsal surface, white on the ventral surface, and silver on the sides. Transformed eels migrate back to the Sargasso Sea where they spawn, beginning the cycle again.

More than 100 species of mullet, another type of catadromous fish, live in temperate and tropical estuaries. Striped mullet (*Mugil cephalus*) are large, reaching maximum lengths of 47.2 inches (120 cm) and weights of 17.6 pounds (8 kg). Each striped mullet is olive to brown dorsally, with green or blue sides that fade into a white belly. Dark lines run the length of the body laterally.

During the day, adults feed over sandy or vegetated estuary floors. Schools of mullet suck up the top layer of sediment, filtering out the nutritious, bacteria-covered detritus, microalgae, and small crustaceans. Mullet also graze on the small plants and animals that grow on sea grasses, and they consume the mucus scum that forms at the air-water interface.

Mullet spawn at sea in late summer or early fall, with males and females shedding gametes in the water. Fertilized eggs float to the sea's surface, buoyed by drops of oil. After 48 hours, the eggs hatch into larvae that swim into shallow regions of the estuary where food is plentiful and plant cover provides protection from predators. When mullet are about 2 inches (5 cm) in length, they move to slightly deeper water to mature. By three to five years of age, they join other sexually mature adults in offshore spawning events.

Mudskippers, Weakfish, and Bluefish

One of the most unusual groups of bony fish are the amphibious mudskippers that live in estuaries of Africa, the Indian Ocean, Indonesia, and Australia. Measuring only about four to six inches (10 to 15.2 cm) long, these animals are literally "fish out of water" that spend more time on the mud flats of the estuary than they do in the water. To emerge on land, these unique fish haul their bodies up and out of the water with pectoral fins that are modified as muscular forelimbs. A mudskipper can coordinate movements of the forelimbs with its ventral fins to "walk" around on the mud. With powerful flips of its tail, the fish can hop across an area with enough speed to avoid predators.

In the water, a mudskipper breathes with gills like other fish, but when it is out of water, the fish breathes air through its damp gills. To keep its gills moist, a mudskipper must carry a mouthful of water. If the fish opens its mouth to catch prey, the water runs out and must be replaced immediately. Mudskippers can also absorb some supplemental oxygen through their moist skin.

One of the most common mudskippers is *Periophthalmus argentilineatus,* a dull-colored animal that is brownish gray dorsally with dark bands on its sides. This species not only leaves the water, but also climbs mangrove trees in search of food. To keep its skin moist on extended forays on land, the mudskipper rolls around in the mud to coat its body, then wipes mud out of its large, prominently located eyes with its pectoral fin.

A mudskipper's eyes sit on top of its head instead of on the sides of the head as in other fish. Eyes in this position can act as periscopes when the fish's body is submerged in water or mud. The eyes move independently of one another, a mechanism that allows the animal to watch for predators approaching from all directions. To keep its eyes moist, the fish rolls them back in their sockets periodically.

Male mudskippers build burrows that have chimneylike towers, structures that help draw air into the underground homes. Male and female fish are identical in appearance, but during breeding season the male develops bright colors on its dorsal fins, chin, and throat. To display these colors and attract a mate, the male does attention-getting push-ups with its pectoral fins. If this is not enough to impress a female, the male leaps several inches into the air, spreads his dorsal fins at the height of the leap, then falls back into the mud. A female who is interested in this display will follow the male back to his burrow to mate. The eggs are fertilized internally, then laid in the lower part of the nest and guarded by the mother.

The lifestyles of mudskippers are the exception and not the rule. Most fish, like the weakfish (*Cynoscion acoupa*), spend their entire lives submerged. Along the eastern coast of the United States, weakfish live along the edges of estuarine grass beds, where they swim in bottom-hugging schools, feeding on shrimp and other small crustaceans. Some of the weakfish's favorite areas are salt marshes and the muddy or sandy bottoms near river mouths.

Weakfish spawn in the estuary, and their young remain there from spring until fall, using it as a nursery. Juvenile fish leave the protected waters and swim to the ocean. Within just two years, weakfish reach sexual maturity—a younger age than many other species of fish. Since they can live to be 17 years or older, early sexual maturation enables weakfish to be reproductively active for 90 percent of their lives. Spawning season lasts for several months, during which time spawning may occur every day.

Bluefish (*Pomatomus saltatrix*), also called choppers or snappers, inhabit the Atlantic coastal estuaries from Nova Scotia to Texas. Schools of bluefish are quite large and may cover tens of square miles off the coast. Feeding on almost any kind of fish, these predators grow to 51 inches (130 cm) and weigh up to 20 pounds (9 kg). Like weakfish, they mature at a young age and may live up to 12 years, giving them many years of reproductive activity.

Drums, Seatrout, and Bass

A red drum (*Sciaenops ocellatus*), or channel bass, can be easily recognized in the estuary by its coppery color and the large black spot at the base of its tail. Growing up to five feet (1.5 m) in length, these impressive fish may weigh up to 75 pounds (34 kg). Red drums are remarkably long-lived, and specimens that are over 55 years of age have been found. Schools of adult red drums migrate to warmer, more southern waters during the winter. Males are able to generate low frequency sounds, called drumming, that may be part of their reproductive signaling. Males reach sexual maturity at one year; females at four or five. Spawning occurs just off the coast three to 10 times per season. During each event, female red drums produce one to three million eggs. Newly hatched larvae are carried into the estuary by wind and currents, and young fish spend eight months feeding and growing in its secure waters.

A full-time resident is the spotted seatrout (*Cynoscion nebulosus*). This long fish is gray dorsally and silver laterally, with bluish highlights. Young fish stay in the safe grass beds where they feed on shrimp and crustaceans, but older fish swim throughout the estuary, pursuing shrimp and other kinds of fish. Spotted seatrout are found from Cape Cod to Mexico.

Among the estuary fish, the black sea bass (*Centropristis striata*) has an unusual life cycle. Sexually, all black sea bass begin life as females, but after they mature, some of the largest animals transform to males. Adults, which are blue-black in color with pale blue or white at the center of each scale, may grow to two feet (61 cm) in length and live up to 20 years. During cold weather, they migrate to warmer waters, returning to the estuaries in the spring.

Flatfish, Seahorses, and Pipefish

Estuaries are homes to fish with unusual body shapes. Flounder are flatfish that live on the estuary floor. In adults, both eyes are located on one side of the head, enabling the fish to watch for prey such as small fish, worms, and crustaceans from hiding places in the sediment. Flounder are well camouflaged on the silty estuary floor with coloration that blends so perfectly that they are very difficult to detect. If a flounder moves from brown soil to an area covered in broken, white shells, its body color changes to match the shells. In fact the flounder is so adept at changing colors that researchers have laid checkerboards on aquaria floor only to find that flounder can mimic the checkered pattern to an amazing degree.

Summer flounder (*Paralichthys dentatus*), or flukes, live in estuaries during summer months but move to deep offshore waters in winter and fall. Like all flounders, their bodies are extremely flattened. After offshore spawning in the fall or winter, larvae move into the estuary. In the larval stage, summer flounder have symmetrically arranged eyes, with one on each side of the head. As they metamorphose to the post-larval stage, one eye slowly migrates until both eyes are located on the left side of the head. Once the eyes are in position, a young flounder takes its place in the sediment, lying on its right side with other adults. At maturity, one year for males and two for females, spawning occurs in the fall. Adults can reach weights of 26 pounds (11.8 kg), but an average weight is 6 pounds (2.7 kg) and an average length 22 inches (8.6 cm).

Winter flounder (*Pleuronectes americanus*) live a similar lifestyle but differ from summer flounder in that their eyes and mouth migrate to the right side of the head. Starry flounder (*Platichthys stellatus*) are ambidextrous flatfish that may develop both eyes on either the right or the left side of their heads. In California, 50 percent of the starry flounder are right-eyed and 50 percent are left-eyed.

More than 32 species of seahorses live in temperate and tropical estuarine waters. Seahorses favor the warm, shallow-water areas, as well as the zones around sea grass beds or mangrove roots. Named for the horselike shape of their heads, seahorses are extremely atypical fish. The skin on their scaleless bodies is stretched over bony plates. When they swim, seahorses move through the water in an upright position instead of leading with their heads, like most other kinds of fish. Earlike pectoral fins steer them, and they are propelled by their dorsal fins. To maintain a stationary position in the water, seahorses wrap their prehensile tails around vegetation. Narrow snouts work much like straws, sucking in small particles of food suspended in the water.

During breeding season, the female seahorse lays about 200 eggs in a pouch that is situated on her mate's abdomen. Eggs attach to the spongy interior wall of the pouch and are fertilized by the father's sperm. After two to six weeks, hatchlings begin to emerge. Instead of all babies appearing at the same time, hatchlings swim from the pouch over a period of two days. Young seahorses do not receive care or protection from their parents and are vulnerable to predators.

A close relative of the seahorse is the cylindrically shaped pipefish. Although they have horselike heads similar to those of seahorses, the bodies of pipefish resemble eight- to 12-inch (20.3- to 30.5-cm) long pencils. Pipefish lack pelvic fins and use their dorsal fins for swimming. As in seahorses, the pectoral fins of pipefish are located near the head and resemble ears. These fish lie on the bottom of the estuary, where their black coloration helps them blend in to the surroundings. Sometimes they move to beds of eelgrass, changing colors to match the grasses. Instead of smooth skin, pipefish are covered with armored scales for protection. Males have large brood pouches where eggs develop.

Oyster Toadfish and Common Toadfish

Pipefish and seahorses are small and almost dainty animals, but the oyster toadfish (*Opsanus tau*) is described by some biologists as big and ugly. The toadfish's 12-inch (30.5-cm) long body is brownish, and its enormous mouth is filled with blunt teeth. Large, protruding eyes, a short snout, whisker-like projections around its jaws, sharp gill covers, and spiny protrusions on its cheeks give the fish a bizarre expression. In addition, the scaleless skin is covered with a layer of mucus.

As year-round residents of estuaries on the eastern coast of the United States, oyster toadfish hide in muddy bottoms, waiting to ambush prey. Not picky eaters, they will consume almost anything that comes their way. Mollusks, crustaceans, squid, and fish are just some of the animals preyed on by oyster toadfish.

During breeding season, males attract females with a grunting sound. Both males and females are capable of generating this sound and will do so if threatened by a predator. Spawning takes place for several months, beginning in the spring and ending in mid-fall. The male locates and secures a nesting place, then the female swims in and lays large, sticky eggs. After fertilizing the eggs, the male displays *territorial behavior*, standing guard for about a month. As the young fish mature, they stay in the immediate vicinity, never wandering far from their parents. As a result, populations of oyster toad-fish are not very efficient at increasing their range.

An unrelated group of fish with a similar name are the toadfish or puffers, such as the common toadfish (*Tetractenos hamiltoni*), a resident of Australian estuaries. Whitish in color, the common toadfish is covered with spots on its back and sides and with brown blotches on its belly. A small mouth holds teeth that are fused to form a beak-like structure, an efficient instrument for cracking the shells of crabs.

A common toadfish may swim in schools or spend the day buried in sand with only its eyes protruding. When the tide goes out, some toadfish deliberately strand themselves on mud flats so they can feed on the crabs there. To stay moist while out of water, they carve out shallow nests in the mud and wait for their prey. When the tide returns, the toadfish ride it back into the estuary.

The common toadfish shares characteristics with other members of its family, the Tetradontidae. All members of this group have blunt, club-shaped bodies that lack pelvic fins and move slowly in the water. To protect themselves from preda-tors, toadfish enlarge their bodies by swallowing huge quanti-ties of water and holding it in stretchable sections of their stomachs. Inflating makes these relatively small fish look much larger and fiercer, a deterrent to some predators. In addition, a puffed-up fish is much more difficult for a preda-tor to swallow than a smooth one.

The toadfish's best protection may be the deadly toxin, tetrodotoxin, in its tissues. Most concentrated in its liver and eggs, the toxin can be found in smaller concentrations in the skin and other tissues. Tetrodotoxin is a poison that interferes with the transmission of nerve impulses to muscles. As a result, it slows, or even stops, the muscles of the heart and res-piratory system. Immediately after eating puffer toxin, a per-son may feel dizzy and uncoordinated. Sweating and weakness follow, then a decrease in blood pressure and numbness in fin-gers and toes. Paralysis, convulsions, and death can result.

Conclusion

Fish are the most common vertebrates in the estuarine system. Although all types of fish are highly adapted for life in the water, different species are specialized for particular feeding styles. Fish in the estuary may be part-time or full-time residents, depending on their life cycles.

Sharks and rays are primitive fish whose skeletons are made of cartilage. Rays, like the Atlantic stingray, are rounded, flattened bottom-feeders. Sharks are more torpedo-shaped cartilaginous fish. In an estuary, one might see several species of sharks, among them leopard sharks and hammerheads. Like most sharks, these animals are active predators that can be found hunting alone or in small groups.

Bony fish are by far the largest group of estuarine fish. Those that travel from freshwater to salt water to lay their eggs are known as anadromous fish and include the American shad, Atlantic menhaden, several species of salmon, striped bass, and Atlantic sturgeon. Most of these fish travel to the mouth of the estuary to lay and fertilize their eggs. Hatchlings float or swim into the estuary, where they feed on the rich supply of food and find protection from predators among the dense plant life. As adults, they return to the ocean. American eels and mullet are catadromous fish that live most of their lives in freshwater but travel to saltwater for spawning. American eels exhibit a complex life cycle that involves several phases of development.

Some of the fish found in estuaries have unusual adaptations. Mudskippers are small, tropical fish that spend more time out of the water than in it. Like many of their relatives, mudskippers are able to keep their gills moist and use oxygen in the air. To hoist themselves out of the water and move across the mud, they use highly modified and quite muscular fins.

Flatfish, like flounder, are oddly shaped animals that lie quietly on the bottom of the estuary waiting for suitable prey to swim close. Because flounder spend their entire lives on the bottom, their bodies are flat and both of their eyes, as well as their mouth, are located on one side of the head. This arrangement prevents the fish from having to raise its head to view its surroundings, an adaptation that keeps it from giving away its position. In addition, flounder can change color, depending on the substrate on which they are lying.

Bass, trout, weakfish, and a host of other species make their homes in the estuary. All of these organisms are able to tolerate a wide range of salinities. Estuary fish benefit from a rich supply of food and a relatively safe environment. For most commercial species of fish, and even those with no commercial value, estuaries play essential roles in development in growth.

6

Reptiles, Birds, and Mammals
Air-Breathing Animals of the Saltwater Wetland

Although fish are the most numerous vertebrates in estuaries, these ecosystems also serve as homes, nurseries, and resting places for a variety of other animals with backbones. A wide range of *birds*, *reptiles*, and *mammals* play important roles in the food chains of the estuaries. In addition, countless terrestrial and freshwater vertebrates interact with the estuary along its borders. The list of species is staggering,

Marine Reptile Anatomy

Reptiles are not usually associated with marine environments. In fact, of the 6,000 known species of reptiles, only about 1 percent inhabits the sea. Members of this select group include lizards, crocodiles, turtles, and snakes. Each of these organisms shares many of the same anatomical structures that are found in all reptiles: They are cold-blooded, air-breathing, scaled animals that reproduce by internal fertilization. Yet, to live in salt water, this subgroup has evolved some special adaptations not seen in terrestrial reptiles.

In turtles, the shell is the most unique feature. The lightweight, streamline shape of the shell forms a protective enclosure for the vital organs. The ribs and backbone of the turtle are securely attached to the inside of the shell. The upper part of the shell, the

carapace, is covered with horny plates that connect to the shell's bottom, the plastron. Extending out from the protective shell are the marine turtle's legs, which have been modified into paddle-like flippers capable of propelling it at speeds of up to 35 miles per hour (56 kph) through the water. These same legs are cumbersome on land, making the animals slow and their movements awkward.

Most air-breathing vertebrates cannot drink salty water because it causes dehydration and kidney damage. Seawater contains sodium chloride and other salts in concentrations three times greater than blood and body fluids. Many marine reptiles drink seawater, so their bodies rely on special salt-secreting glands to handle the excess salt. To reduce the load of salt in body fluids,

but this chapter focuses on some of the most common estuarine vertebrates and those that can only survive in estuaries.

Although very few reptiles spend their entire lives in brackish water environments, two that do are the saltwater crocodile and diamondback turtle. The imposing saltwater, or Indo-Pacific, crocodiles (*Crocodylus porosus*) make their homes in brackish waters throughout tropical Asia and the Pacific. Living from 70 to 100 years, the reptiles can reach lengths of 7.5 feet (2.9 m) to 11 feet (3.4 m).

A saltwater crocodile is equipped with several adaptations for its marine lifestyle. Protective flaps and scales cover the nostrils and eardrums when the animal dives. Clear eyelids protect the eyes during dives and underwater battles yet permit the crocodile to see where it is going. To cope with the

these glands produce and excrete fluid that is twice as salty as seawater. The glands work very quickly, processing and getting rid of salt about 10 times faster than kidneys. Salt glands are located on the head, often near the eyes.

There are more than 50 species of sea snakes that thrive in marine environments. Sea snakes possess adaptations such as nasal valves and close-fitting scales around the mouth that keep water out during diving. Flattened tails that look like small paddles easily propel these reptiles through the water. The lungs in sea snakes are elongated, muscular air sacs that are able to store oxygen. In addition, sea snakes can take in oxygen through the skin. Their adaptations to the marine environment enable sea snakes to stay submerged from 30 minutes up to two hours; however, this ability comes at a cost. Because marine snakes routinely swim to the surface to breathe, they use more energy and have higher metabolic rates than land snakes. To balance their high energy consumption, they require more food than their terrestrial counterparts.

Finally, crocodiles usually occupy freshwater, but there are some species that live in brackish water (in between salt water and freshwater) and salt water. These animals have salivary glands that have been modified to excrete salt. Their tails are flattened for side-to-side swimming and their toes possess well-developed webs. Saltwater crocodiles are equipped with valves at the back of the throat that enable them to open their mouths and feed underwater without flooding their lungs.

high salinity of its environment, an estuarine crocodile has a salt-excreting gland on its tongue.

An opportunistic predator, the saltwater crocodile's diet varies with its maturity level as well as its specific location. Young crocodiles normally dine on small crustaceans like shrimp and crabs, as well as a variety of insects. As the reptiles become juveniles, meals begin to include vertebrates such as fish, snakes, and birds. Mature crocodiles lay in wait for larger marine prey such as turtles and sharks, as well as mammals that come too close to the edge of the water. In a few cases, adult crocodiles have attacked cattle and humans. A crocodile kills its prey either by drowning it or by shaking its head back and forth violently to break the victim's bones. When the prey is dead, the crocodile swallows it whole.

Most saltwater crocodiles breed between November and March. A female constructs a large nesting mound from mud and bits of plant material, then deposits 40 to 60 leathery eggs. For the next three weeks, she stays nearby to guard her eggs. When the tiny crocodiles are fully developed, they break out of their shells with their egg teeth, special teeth located on the tops of their snouts just for opening eggs. The mother alligator gently scoops up her offspring in her mouth and carries them to the water.

Turtles

The diamondback turtle (*Malaclemys terrapin*) is a semiaquatic reptile whose habitat is limited to the brackish waters of estuarine environments. Active only from spring to fall, this reptile copes with cold weather by hibernating in the mud. Clams, crabs, snails, and some marsh plants make up the terrapin's diet. The feet and legs of diamondback turtles are shaped like those of land turtles, except for the fact that the hind legs are larger and more powerful, an adaptation that enables the turtles to swim efficiently in the energetic tidal waters that flow through estuaries.

The female diamondback turtle, like the one in the lower color insert on page C-8, may grow to 7.5 inches (19 cm), while the male is usually smaller. In both sexes, the shell is light gray, brown, or black, with edges of yellow to olive, and etched with deep-cut diamond shapes. The turtles' skin is whitish with black marks on it. Females become reproductively active between eight and 13 years of age. During the spring, turtles mate. The sperm deposited inside the female's body is stored until eggs are produced, at which time they are fertilized. At egg-laying time, a female leaves the estuarine water and travels to a sandy beach or dune, where she digs a six-inch (15.2-cm) deep nest for her fertilized eggs, as shown in the lower color insert on page C-5. After 60 to 120 days, the hatchlings emerge and scramble for the water.

Unlike the diamondback turtle, sea turtles are full-time marine reptiles. The limbs of sea turtles are modified as strong flippers for swimming. Like other reptiles, sea turtles are air breathers, so when active, they may surface every few minutes. During periods of rest in underwater caves or on ledges, they can remain submerged for as much as two and a half hours.

After hatching, young sea turtles swim in the open ocean for a few years. When they reach a certain size, which varies with species, turtles leave the ocean and move to nearshore environments like beaches and estuaries. Most common in estuaries during spring and summer when food is abundant, sea turtles feast on submerged macroalgae and sea grasses as well as invertebrates. Some of the sea turtles that spend time in estuaries include green turtles (*Chelonia mydas*), loggerhead turtles (*Caretta caretta*), Atlantic hawksbill sea turtles (*Eretmochelys imbricata*), Kemp's ridley turtles (*Lepidochelys kempii*), and leatherback turtles (*Dermochelys coriacea*).

The green sea turtle grows to lengths of 2.5 to 3.4 feet (0.76 to 1.1 m) and weighs between 200 and 400 pounds (90.7 to 181.4 kg). Compared to other sea turtles, the green sea turtle has a relatively small head. Its large carapace is mottled with shades of dark brown on top but is creamy white below.

Green sea turtles, which can live to be 80 years old, mature slowly and do not reach sexual maturity until they are 25 years old. Every two or three years, mature turtles make long journeys to mate and lay their eggs, leaving their tropical feeding grounds and swimming 600 miles or more to return to the beaches where they were born. During the months of

March and April, turtles mate in offshore waters, then females go ashore to lay their eggs.

A female selects a spot above the tide line where she can dig an egg chamber with her powerful hind legs. Once a chamber is complete, the female lays 100 to 200 small eggs, covers them with sand, and returns to the sea. Sixty days later, the hatchlings emerge and race to the water. Green sea turtles remain at sea for several years, feeding on jellyfish and other invertebrates. They return to estuaries and other nearshore regions when they are juveniles.

Loggerhead turtles, like the one in the upper color insert on page C-6, are named for their large heads, which can be 10 inches (25.4 cm) across. Reaching lengths of three feet (1 m) and weights of 400 pounds (182 kg), loggerheads have heart-shaped shells that are reddish brown in color. Found in the Atlantic Ocean, loggerheads range from Argentina to Newfoundland as

Fig. 6.1 Hawksbill sea turtles may visit estuaries to feed. (Courtesy of Florida Keys National Marine Sanctuary, NOAA)

well as into the Gulf of Mexico and the Caribbean and Mediterranean Seas.

One of the largest species of sea turtles is the leatherback sea turtle. Unlike other turtles, the shell of the leatherback is not bony but made of leathery hide. Leatherbacks can reach lengths of seven feet (2 m) and weigh as much as 1,500 pounds (680 kg).

Two slightly smaller sea turtles are the Atlantic hawksbill, named for its hawk-shaped jaw, and the Kemp's ridley. The carapace of the adult Atlantic hawksbill, featured in Figure 6.1, is orange, brown, and yellow, while hatchlings are brown with pale blotches. Kemp's ridley sea turtle is covered with a carapace that is olive green dorsally and light green ventrally.

Birds of the Estuary

Estuaries provide homes, havens, or rest stops for a wide variety of birds. Many, such as some species of sparrows, egrets, and cormorants, are year-round residents who build nests and spend their entire lives in the estuarine system. Hundreds of other species, including terns, herons, pelicans, and vireos, visit the estuaries to build their nests or simply to rest during migratory trips.

An estuary is able to support a large number of birds because each species specializes in a particular feeding niche. As a result, different kinds of birds can use the same food resources without direct competition. Feeding specializations can be seen in beaks, feet, and legs. Beaks may be designed for jobs such as cracking nuts, filtering algae from water, probing for worms, and digging up shells, while feet and legs are modified for swimming, running, walking, or diving. Although every estuary houses a unique community of birds, some of the most prominent families found in brackish water environments worldwide include: herons and egrets (Ardeidae); swans, geese, and ducks (Anatidae); ibis and spoonbills (Threskiornithidae); pelicans (Pelecanidae); stilts and avocets (Recurvirostridae); gulls (Laridae); plovers (Charadriidae); oystercatchers (Haematopodidae); cormorants (Phalacrocoracidae); ospreys (Panlionidae); rails (Rallidae); sandpipers (Scolopacidae); and skimmers (Rynchopidae).

Marine Bird Anatomy

Birds are warm-blooded vertebrates that have feathers to insulate and protect their bodies. In most species of birds, feathers are also important adaptations for flying. As a general rule, birds devote a lot of time and energy to keeping their feathers waterproof in a process called preening. During preening, birds rub their feet, feathers, and beaks with oil produced by the preen gland near their tail.

The strong, lightweight bones of birds are especially adapted for flying. Many of the bones are fused, resulting in the rigid type of skeleton needed for flight. Although birds are not very good at tasting or smelling, their senses of hearing and sight are exceptional. They maintain a constant, relatively high body temperature and a rapid rate of metabolism. To efficiently pump blood around their bodies, they have a four-chambered heart.

Like marine reptiles, marine birds have glands that remove excess salt from their bodies. Although the structure and purpose of the salt gland is the same in all marine birds, its location varies by species. In most marine birds, salt accumulates in a gland near the nostrils and then oozes out of the bird's body through the nasal openings.

The term *seabird* is not scientific but is used to describe a wide range of birds whose lifestyles are associated with the ocean. Some seabirds never get further out into the ocean than the surf water. Many seabirds are equipped with adaptations of their bills, legs, and feet. Short, tweezerlike bills can probe for animals that are near the surface of the sand or mud, while long, slender bills reach animals that burrow deeply. Several styles of seabird bills are shown in Figure 6.2. For wading on wet soil, many seabirds have lobed feet, while those who walk through mud or shallow water have long legs and feet with wide toes.

Other marine birds are proficient swimmers and divers who have special adaptations for spending time in water. These include wide bodies that have good underwater stability, thick layers of body fat for buoyancy, and dense plumage for warmth. In swimmers, the legs are usually located near the posterior end of the body to allow for easy maneuvers, and the feet have webs or lobes between the toes.

All marine birds must come to the shore to breed and lay their eggs. Breeding grounds vary from rocky ledges to sandy beaches. More than 90 percent of marine birds are colonial and require the social stimulation of other birds to complete the breeding process. Incubation of the eggs varies from one species to the next, but as a general rule the length of incubation correlates to the size of the egg: Large eggs take longer to hatch than small ones do.

Bills of Shorebirds

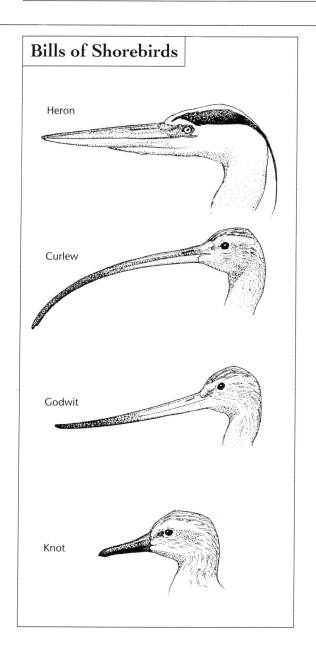

Heron

Curlew

Godwit

Knot

*Fig. 6.2   The bills of shorebirds are adapted
for a variety of feeding styles.*

The herons of the Ardeidae family are tall birds with long, slender necks, legs, and beaks. Standing three feet (0.91 m) tall, with wingspans of 6 feet (1.8 m), these animals walk through the shallow water with a stately bearing. To manage their gangly bodies in flight, the birds fold back their necks, hunch down their heads, and let their legs trail straight behind.

Herons are supreme hunters whose height gives them an advantage when searching for shallow-water prey. They may stand motionless for long periods of time waiting to ambush a fish or crab, or they can walk through the water, stirring it to flush out small animals. When hunting, a heron bends its neck into an S shape, then quickly uncoils it to stab prey.

Like many types of birds, herons follow ritualized courtship behaviors, some of which are quite spectacular. Some species develop lacey plumage on their heads, breasts, and backs during mating season. In others, coloration of the legs, bills, eyes, and lores (patches of skin between the eyes and bill) intensifies. Mating is usually monogamous, and a pair will stay with their nest, alternating egg-sitting duty. Most couples build their nests in large, noisy colonies of herons called heronries.

The great blue heron (*Ardea herodias*) is the largest American species. The adult heron is blue-gray with a white head, yellow beak, and a black streak that extends from behind the eye to the back of the head. The great egret (*Casmerodius albus*), pictured in the lower color insert on page C-6, is a close relative of the heron. These majestic white birds can be found on both the east and west coasts of the United States, near Mexico, and in Central and South America.

Ibises, spoonbills, and their relatives are long-legged wading birds whose slender, stalklike legs end in partly webbed feet. Elongated, downward curving bills are ideal for feeding on small animals, including crustaceans, worms, and fish. The white ibis (*Eudocimus albus*), found from the southern United States to northern South America, is white except for red skin on its face, a red bill and legs, and black tips on its wings. The glossy ibis (*Plegadis falcinellus*) is a smaller bird with dark plumage that sparkles with iridescent greens and purples and green bills and legs. The pink roseate spoonbill (*Ajaia ajaja*) shares a lot of characteristics with ibises but has a distinctive, spatulate bill. By swinging the bill through the water as it wades forward, the roseate spoonbill finds crustaceans, fish, and worms.

Pelicans are an easy group to identify because they have distinctive, pouch-like beaks. These large beaks are capable of holding prey, such as fish or squid, as well as a few gallons of water. Brown pelicans (*Pelecanus occidentalis*), like the one in the upper color insert on page C-7 are typical of the group. Measuring 41 inches (104 cm) in length with a wingspan of 90 inches (228.6 cm), the body of a brown pelican is covered with gray-brown feathers, except for an area around the head where the plumage is white.

A pelican flies low over estuary water, watching for fish. When one is spotted, the pelican goes into a dive, plunging 30 to 60 feet (9.1 to 18.3 m) and hitting the water bill-first. The impact from such a height would be fatal to other birds, but the pelican is equipped with air sacs just beneath the skin that cushion the blow. As the bird opens its mouth to take in the prey, loose skin on the underside of the bill extends to form a scoop that can hold 2.5 to 3 gallons (9.5 to 11.3 L).

A pelican drains the water from its pouch before tossing its head back to swallow the catch.

Stilts and avocets are graceful, long-necked birds with black and white plumage. The reddish legs of stilts and the blue-toned legs of avocets are designed for wading in shallow water. Both kinds of birds feed by moving their beaks through the water, probing for small animals. Avocets have upturned bills; the beaks of stilts are straight.

Black-winged stilts (*Himantopus himantopus*) are familiar sights in the shallow waters of estuaries worldwide. Although they generally stroll and probe the mud for food, they can also swim and dive if necessary. During breeding season, the male carries out elaborate courtship rituals that involve pecking the ground, preening, circling the female, and flicking water on her. Once a mate is confirmed and eggs are laid, black-winged stilts keep the eggs cool during hot weather by soaking their belly feathers with water, then carrying the water to the nest. In extremely hot weather, a pair may make more than 100 trips a day from the water to the nest. If predators threaten, black-winged stilts distract them with a repertoire of acts, including the injured bird charade and the fake nest act.

Gulls are some of the best-known estuarine birds, and most people recognize them by sight. The ring-billed gull (*Laurs delawarensis*) is widespread in North America. Small fish, worms, invertebrates, and small mammals like mice make up the diets of ring-bill gulls, which build their nests on the ground in the grassy marsh. The cry of laughing gulls (*Larus atricilla*), a distinctive "ha-ha-ha-haaaah," is a familiar sound in many brackish wetlands. Growing to about 17 inches (43 cm), breeding adults have black heads and red bills. Like all gulls, laughing gulls are equipped with long, narrow wings for graceful flight as well as webbed feet for powerful swimming. Amid colonies that may include hundreds of gulls, mating pairs find nesting sites in the tall grasses.

Skimmers and scissorbills, relatives of gulls, are small birds, growing to only 20 inches (50 cm) in length. Two of their most distinguishing characteristics are the vertically slit irises of their eyes, which resemble the eyes of cats, and their jutting lower jaws. Like the black skimmer in the lower color insert on page C-7, these birds fly just above the water with their mouths open, skimming its surface with their lower beaks to catch surface-swimming prey.

Plovers, small birds that look a lot like sandpipers, are common from the Arctic to the tropics. A plover's plumage is sandy-colored, accented with a black band across its forehead and a black ring around the base of the neck. Yellow-orange legs contrast sharply to their dull-colored feathers. Unlike most other wading birds, plovers are short in stature. They specialize in feeding along the edges of the water, running and stopping erratically. As the waves recede from shore, plovers follow them, watching for signs of life just below the mud's surface.

American oystercatchers (*Haematopus palliatus*) are gull-sized birds that have black and white feathers, pink legs, and orange bills. Each year during breeding season, lifetime mates build ground nests where the female lays two to four gray eggs. Within 35 days, young chicks are able to fly and start looking for their own food. Oystercatchers chiefly feed on bivalves in the intertidal zone. Instead of swallowing their prey whole, like many birds, they pry open the mollusks with their bills, then eat the flesh within. To get rid of any sand that might cling to their food, oystercatchers swish their meals through the water before swallowing.

The cormorants, in Figure 6.3, are large birds that are mostly black as adults. Their slender beaks end in hooks and, in some species, their long necks are set off by bright, yellow-orange throat patches. Webbed feet and powerful legs enable cormorants to dive for fish and invertebrates, sometimes going as deep as 60 feet (18.3 m). After diving, cormorants sit in the Sun with their wings spread, drying. Because they have no oil glands to waterproof their feathers, drying is an important daily activity for them. A feeding bird captures prey in its bill, brings it to the surface, turns the prey so that it is going down head-first (a strategy that keeps spines from getting stuck in the throat), then swallows. Each day, the birds regurgitate pellets of indigestible fish scales and bones. Like many estuary birds, cormorants are colonial animals that nest in treetops.

Ospreys are eagle-like animals that soar 100 feet above the water looking for prey. Also called fish hawks, these birds are about 21 to 24 inches (53.3 to 60.9 cm) long, with wingspans of 4 to 6 feet (1.2 to 1.8 m). Their wings and backs are brown and their breasts and upper legs white. Breeding adults mate for life and raise their young in nests built offshore.

Rails are chicken-sized, year-round residents of salt marshes. Reaching lengths of up to 16 inches (41 cm), the long-billed bird is grayish brown in color, with black and white barred flanks. Female rails deposit nine to 12 buff-colored eggs in shallow nests constructed of marsh grasses. If a nest needs camouflaging, the parents may add a canopy of sticks and grass. The light-footed clapper rail (*Rallus longirostris levipes*) is a secretive, hard-to-spot estuary resident, although most visitors to the area will recognize its rattling calls, a series of 10 or more "kek kek keks."

Swans, geese, and ducks are migratory waterfowl that share many characteristics. Most have short legs and webbed feet, two adaptations for swimming. All fly with strong, continuous beats of their wings, necks stretched out in front of their

Fig. 6.3 After diving, cormorants spread their wings to dry. (Courtesy of Mary Hollinger, NODC biologist, NOAA)

bodies. Many swans, geese, and ducks visit estuaries because they are on their migration paths or make up part of their wintering habitats.

The San Francisco Bay estuary is one of the major stopovers for ducks, geese, and swans traveling along the Pacific flyway, the path followed by migratory birds on North America's Pacific coast. The canvasback duck (*Aythya valisineria*) prefers the brackish estuarine waters to the fresh waters of the rivers that fill the bay. The male canvasback has a red head, red eyes, white body, and black breast and tail. The female has similar markings, but the colors are muted.

Mammals

Estuaries are important to several marine mammals, including species of whales, porpoises, dolphins, harbor seals, and sea otters. Most of these large animals are estuarine visitors who spend the majority of their lives in other parts of the sea. Mammals are attracted to estuaries during summer months when food production is at its peak and water temperatures are warm. Estuaries provide safe breeding grounds and ideal places to rest and refuel during long, migratory journeys.

Dolphins and whales share many characteristics, and both are classified as cetaceans. Having evolved from animals that lived on land, their bodies share many of the features of terrestrial mammals. However, cetaceans are highly specialized for the aquatic environment. In all members, the front appendages are modified as flippers and, except for vestigial bones in the skeletal structure, the hind ones are absent.

Cetaceans are divided into two large groups, based on their manner of feeding: baleen whales and toothed whales. Baleen whales have enormous mouths that contain huge plates of baleen instead of teeth. Baleen plates, which resemble gigantic combs, enable a cetacean to filter tiny organisms out of the seawater. Toothed whales, a group that includes dolphins and porpoises, have teeth and eat meat.

Cetaceans communicate with one another with low frequency voice sounds that are within the human range of hearing. These sounds vary by species but include vocabularies of clicks and whistles. In addition, the mammals use mechanically produced sounds such as jaw snapping, flipper slapping, and crash dives that may also be communication signals.

Depending on the geographical location, bottlenose dolphins (*Tursiops truncates*), shown in Figure 6.4, congregate in estuaries. Bottlenoses, which are relatively small cetaceans, are the most common and abundant species of dolphin on the eastern coast of the United States. Males can reach lengths of 12.5 feet (3.8 m), although most are smaller. Despite their abundance, the familiar bottlenose is not the only dolphin seen in estuaries. White-beaked dolphins and whitesided dolphins also visit the warm, brackish waters.

Bottlenose dolphins form pods of varying sizes, some small and family-like, while others contain hundreds of individuals. Calves may be born at any time of the year, although they are most likely to be born during warm weather. The gestation period is about a year, and nursing continues for another year. The average life span of a bottlenose dolphin is about 45 years.

Fig. 6.4   Bottlenose dolphins are residents of estuaries. (Courtesy of Getty Images)

Marine Mammal Anatomy

Mammals are warm-blooded vertebrates that have hair and breathe air. All females of this group have milk-producing mammary glands with which to feed their young. Mammals also have a diaphragm that pulls air into the lungs and a four-chambered heart for efficient circulation of blood. The teeth of mammals are specialized by size and shape for particular uses.

Marine mammals are subdivided into four categories: cetaceans, animals that spend their entire lives in the ocean; sirenians, herbivorous ocean mammals; pinnipeds, web-footed mammals; and marine otters. Animals in all four categories have the same characteristics as terrestrial mammals, as well as some special adaptations that enable them to survive in their watery environment.

The cetaceans, which include whales, dolphins, and porpoises, have stream-lined bodies, horizontal tail flukes, and paddle-like flippers that enable them to move quickly through the water. Layers of blubber (subcutaneous fat) insulate their bodies and act as storage places for large quantities of energy. Their noses (blowholes) are located on the tops of their heads so air can be inhaled as soon as the organism surfaces above the water.

Manatees and dugongs are the only sirenians. These docile, slow-moving herbivores lack a dorsal fin or hind limbs but are equipped with front limbs that move at the elbow, as well as with a flattened tail. Their powerful tails propel them through the water, while the front limbs act as paddles for steering.

The pinnipeds—seals, sea lions, and walruses—are carnivores that have webbed feet. Although very awkward on land, the pinnipeds are agile and aggressive hunters in the water. This group of marine mammals is protected from the cold by hair and blubber. During deep-water dives, their bodies are able to restrict blood flow to vital organs and slow their heart rates to only a few beats a minute, strategies that reduce oxygen consumption. All pinnipeds come onto land or ice at breeding time.

The sea otters spend their entire lives at sea and only come ashore during storms. They are much smaller than the other marine mammals. Even though otters are very agile swimmers and divers, they are clumsy on shore. Their back feet, which are flipperlike and fully webbed, are larger than their front feet. Internally, their bodies are adapted to deal with the salt in seawater with enlarged kidneys that can eliminate the excess salt.

Several species of whales spend summer months in estuaries. The species present and the length of their stay depend on geographic location. For example, from June through

October, the St. Lawrence River estuary hosts beluga, blue, fin back, minke, humpback, and sperm whales.

Beluga whales (*Delphinapterus leucas*), easily identified by their solid white color, breed in the spring before migrating to estuaries. Belugas remain in the estuaries all summer, giving birth to their young and feasting on fish and shellfish. Gestation lasts for 14 months, so the calves born in August were conceived two springs earlier. When fall arrives, all of the whales migrate to the Arctic Ocean.

Belugas are very social animals that live in close-knit pods. In estuaries, aggregate can grow to immense sizes, building to thousands of animals. To communicate with one another, the mammals use diverse whistles and squeaks; sounds that may employ the inflated areas called melons that are located on their heads.

Humpback whales (*Megaptera novaengliae*) are impressive animals that reach 53 feet (16.2 m) in length. These baleen whales visit estuaries along the Atlantic coast from Iceland to the West Indies and Gulf of Mexico, and in the Pacific Ocean from the Bering Sea to southern Mexico. The flippers of humpbacks are longer than those of other whales, often one-third of the whales' body length. Covering the upper and lower jaws are bumpy tubercles, each containing a hairlike structure, a vibrissa, which detects vibrations in the water. The throat, a large area running from the tip of the lower jaw to the naval, is made up of grooved skin that is folded in pleats. When the whale opens its mouth, the pleats unfold, allowing the animal to expand the size of its bite to three times its normal width.

Humpback whales carry out much of their communication through songs. Within a population of whales, all of the males begin the breeding season singing the same song. As the season progresses, each male changes his version so that by the end of a breeding season, all of the songs are distinctly different. The exact function of songs is not known, but they are believed to be associated with mating. For example, some songs may attract females while others warn off other males.

One of the few year-round estuarine residents is the harbor seal. Found in estuaries along the coasts of both the Pacific and Atlantic Oceans of North America, harbor, or common, seals (*Phoca vitulina*) are tan to silver in color, with mottled spots or rings. Harbor seals are medium-size, spindle-shaped animals with rounded heads and doglike muzzles. Males weigh up to 370 pounds (170 kg) and reach lengths of 40 inches (100 cm), but females are slightly smaller. During the spring and summer, they inhabit estuaries and the rivers that feed them.

Unlike some other species of seals, harbor seals do not form large breeding colonies. Instead, small groups assemble in quiet estuaries, sometimes swimming up the adjoining freshwater streams, rivers, and lakes. The only close interpersonal relationships are the ones formed between mothers and pups. Pups are usually born during low tide on the estuary mud banks. Within hours of birth, they are able to swim with their mothers in the estuarine waters. Females nurse their pups for about a month before weaning. In the rich estuarine summer waters, pups primarily eat slow-moving shrimp and other small, bottom-dwelling crustaceans, but adults prefer fish.

Harbor seals spend 85 percent of their time foraging for food. When not feeding, they may rest or "haul out" on the shore and lie with their heads and hind flippers elevated in the "banana-like" position. Seals can also rest in the water, in the "bottling" position, with heads tilted straight back and perpendicular to the surface, giving each the appearance of a floating bottle.

Harbor seals do not migrate regularly but will travel from time to time in search of better feeding grounds. In the winter, when ice is likely to form in estuaries, small groups move farther out to sea. Often, they will be gone for several weeks each seal hunting for food alone.

Conclusion

Vertebrates, animals with backbones, include fish, amphibians, reptiles, birds, and mammals. Although a large number of vertebrates interact with the estuary, especially where it borders terrestrial environments, only a few make it their full-time home. One resident is the Indo-Pacific crocodile, a gigantic reptile that lays in wait underwater until its prey ventures along the water's edge. Before a startled victim can move, the crocodile can grab it with powerful jaws and pull it underwater to drown or snap its neck with vicious shaking.

Less vicious, but no less perfectly adapted for the habitat, are several species of turtles. Unable to survive in freshwater or water with high salinity, the diamondback turtle is only found in and around brackish estuarine systems, its hind legs are unusually muscular, an adaptation that helps the turtle swim in the tidally influenced estuary waters. Green turtles, loggerhead turtles, Atlantic hawksbill sea turtles, Kemp's ridley turtles, and leatherback turtles are more likely to be visitors to the area than residents. These large, migratory animals are highly adapted for swimming, with flippers instead of legs and lightweight shells that are easy to manage in water.

The sheer number of birds that live in, or spend part of their lives around, estuaries is staggering. Birds are attracted to the food supplies, nesting sites, and the relative safety of estuarine environments. Estuarine birds are highly specialized for their feeding styles. Some are long-legged waders who step carefully through the shallow water, looking for small fish and crustaceans. Others fly above the water, plunging in when prey is spotted. Diving birds are physically adapted to endure the impacts delivered by daily crashes into the sea. Ospreys also dive through the air for their food, but when they reach the water's surface, they turn so that their sharp talons can grab the prey. Swimmers have webbed feet and wide bodies that enable them to move gracefully along the surface of the water. Skimmers fly just at the water's surface with their large beaks open, skimming up food.

Mammals in the estuary are a smaller group but noticeable because of their large size. Several species of whales visit estuaries in the summer months when food is plentiful. The beluga whale is a solid white cetacean that uses the estuary as a calving and resting ground. The much-larger humpback whale feeds on small invertebrates and plants in the upper portion of the water column, straining tons of water through its comblike baleen plates. The bottlenose dolphin, a relatively small cetacean, is a common sight in estuaries year-round.

The harbor seal is a full-time estuary resident. Unlike some species of seals that prefer colder climes, harbor seals never migrate north, but stay in one general area year-round. Solitary creatures, these mammals may be seen lying on the shore or resting at the water's surface, but most of their time is spent diving for crustaceans and fish. During winter months, harbor seals may move offshore some distance but never break their ties with the estuary.

Most of the vertebrates who choose the estuary are attracted by its rich plant and animal life as well as its relative safety. This combination of factors makes the estuarine environment a perfect nursery for calving animals as well as a safe resting place for migrants.

7

Life on the Edge

A long the coastline, the unique areas where seawater mixes with freshwater from rivers or streams are estuaries. No two estuaries are exactly alike, and individual systems vary in size, shape, temperature, and salinity. Salinity is one of the most important variables in determining the population of an estuary because it controls the physical and chemical character of the system. Estuaries that receive strong freshwater input tend to have layers of salinity, with the freshwater above and the salt water below. Layers form as a wedge of salty seawater slides into one end of the estuary and pushes its way toward the mouth of the river. On the other hand, estuaries that have weaker freshwater input are dominated by the influence of tides. These types of estuaries are well-mixed and have fairly constant salinity from end to end and from top to bottom.

Most aquatic life-forms are adapted for life in freshwater or salt water, but not both. Only a few, hardy species can tolerate varying salinities. Of those, some are able to thrive in water that is only slightly salty, and others prefer estuarine water that is almost as salty as the sea. Inhabitants of estuaries are exceptional because they possess structural adaptations that help them deal with varying salt levels.

All estuaries are highly productive ecosystems because they are first in line to receive nutrients washing from the land. In addition, estuarine patterns of circulation bring in nutrients from the sea. As a bonus, estuaries support many nitrogen-fixing bacteria that are able to convert atmospheric nitrogen to forms that living things can use. In other ecosystems, nitrogen is often a limiting factor, and if it runs low, it limits the growth and development of organisms.

These abundant supplies of nutrients support rapid photosynthesis. Producers in the estuary include macroalgae as well as photosynthetic protists in the water column and on the sediments. In temperate estuaries, cord grass is an important producer in the salt marshes. The roles of cord grass are carried out by mangroves in more tropical systems.

Energy moving through an estuarine ecosystem does not travel the same path that it follows through a forest or grassland system. Most of the cord grass and mangroves, as well as some of the macroalgae, are not heavily grazed by animals. Instead, these plants enter the food chain when they die. As detritus, they supply energy to the detrital food webs, which in turn support many of the larger organisms in the estuary ecosystem.

Estuaries support more filter-feeding organisms than other marine and freshwater systems because of their dense populations of green protists. There are so many single-celled photosynthesizers in the water column that zooplankton cannot consume them all. As a result, the green cells fall to the estuary floor where they are picked up by filter feeders such as oysters and clams. In some estuary systems, the populations of filter feeders are so large that all of the water in the system flows over their gills every few days. In the North Inlet Estuary of South Carolina, oysters are able to filter 68 percent of the water that enters the inlet with each high tide.

The Human Factor

Because of the locations, estuaries are more vulnerable to the activities of humans than many other marine ecosystems. Humans have found estuaries to be good places to build seaports and industries that depend on shipping. The constant movement of commercial and private boats through estuarine systems has taken a toll on the life-forms there.

One growing problem is the introduction of alien, or non-native, species that expand their natural ranges by hitching rides on ships. In many cases, an alien species that finds its way into an estuary is able to out-compete the native organisms already living there. As a result, the alien species flourishes and the natives die. Ninety percent of the organisms living in San Francisco Bay are non-native species.

Because of heavy human use, estuaries are vulnerable to other types of damage. Sewage, water from street surfaces, spills of toxic chemicals, air pollutants, and a host of other human-generated chemicals find their way into estuarine waters. All of these factors alter the quality of the water and affect the organisms that live there.

Estuaries are also impacted by humans living far upstream from them. The construction of dams to divert rivers for use as drinking water reduces the amount of freshwater entering estuaries. For example, the Chattahoochee River, which runs between Georgia and Alabama to the Apalachicola Bay in Florida, is caught in the middle of a tristate water war. Georgia and Alabama want to divert the river's water to meet the needs of growing cities such as Birmingham and Atlanta. Florida wants to ensure that the freshwater input to the Apalachicola Bay is not compromised. After years of discussion, the argument is still being negotiated.

Help in the Future

At one time, estuaries and their surrounding wetlands were viewed as wastelands. To make them "usable," the wet regions were drained, dredged, or filled. In the United States, one-third of all the estuaries have already been lost to such short-sighted practices. Increased awareness of the environmental issues associated with estuaries is helping many people understand their important roles. As a result, estuaries are receiving more consideration now than they ever have in the past.

Estuaries have both commercial and intrinsic value. Commercially, they provide jobs for shrimpers, crabbers, and fisherman. The land bordering estuaries is valuable real estate that attracts home and business builders. As tourist attractions, estuarine systems serve as vacation getaways for fishermen and beachcombers.

The intrinsic value of estuaries may be their most important aspect. The very presence of an estuary acts as a filter that catches nutrients, sediments, and even pollution, preventing them from moving further into the environment. As a result, estuaries help improve the quality of water. In addition, they act as buffers between ocean storms and cities, protecting the inland areas from damage. The wetlands also dissipate flood-waters, reducing their harmful effects, and supporting unique populations of organisms.

In recognition of their importance, legislation such as the Estuary and Clean Waters Act of 2000 was designed to protect the estuaries that still exist. Besides developing a national strategy for estuary habitat restoration, the act calls for research and monitoring of estuarine systems. Other programs call for the removal of dams and other impediments that reduce the influx of fresh water, as well as structures that interfere with the tidal flow. In some cases, layers of deep sediments that are filling relatively young estuaries are being removed. Where needed, volunteers plant new stands of cord grass to encourage the plant to once again take up its natural role in the estuary system. To attract wildlife, bird decoys are being placed in shallow water.

Repairing and restoring are essential, but the greatest gift that humans can give themselves and these ecosystems is to prevent further damage. Awareness and education are the keys to saving estuarine systems around the world. These environments have played important environmental and cultural roles in the past, and with care, can continue to do so in the future.

Glossary

A

algal bloom   The rapid growth of cyanobacteria or algae populations that results in large mats of organisms floating in the water.

amphibian   A cold-blooded, soft-skinned vertebrate whose eggs hatch into larvae that metamorphose into adults.

animal   An organism capable of voluntary movement that consumes food rather than manufacturing it from carbon compounds.

anterior   The region of the body that is related to the front or head end of an organism.

appendage   A structure that grows from the body of an organism, such as a leg or antenna.

arthropod   An invertebrate animal that has a segmented body, joined appendages, and chitinous exoskeleton.

asexual reproduction   A type of reproduction that employs means other than the union of an egg and sperm. Budding and binary fission are forms of asexual reproduction.

autotroph   An organism that can capture energy to manufacture its own food from raw materials.

B

binary fission   A type of cell division in monerans in which the parent cell separates into two identical daughter cells.

biodiversity   The number and variety of life-forms that exist in a given area.

bird   A warm-blooded vertebrate that is covered with feathers and reproduces by laying eggs.

bladder   In macroalgae, an inflatable structure that holds gases and helps keep blades of the plant afloat.

blade   The part of a nonvascular plant that is flattened and leaflike.

brood   A type of behavior that enables a parent to protect eggs or offspring as they develop.

budding   A type of asexual reproduction in which an offspring grows as a protrusion from the parent.

buoyancy   The upward force exerted by a fluid on matter that causes the matter to tend to float.

117

C

carnivore   An animal that feeds on the flesh of other animals.

chanocyte   A flagellated cell found in the gastrovascular cavity of a sponge that moves water move through the pores, into the gastrovascular cavity, and out the osculum (an exit for outflow).

chitin   A tough, flexible material that forms the exoskeletons of arthropods and cell walls of fungi.

chlorophyll   A green pigment, found in all photosynthetic organisms, that is able to capture the Sun's energy.

cilia   A microscopic, hairlike cellular extension that can move rhythmically and may function in locomotion or in sweeping food particles toward an animal's mouth or oral opening.

cnidarian   An invertebrate animal that is radially symmetrical and has a saclike internal body cavity and stinging cells.

cnidocyte   A nematocyst-containing cell found in the tentacles of cnidarians that is used to immobilize prey or defend against predators.

countershading   One type of protective, two-tone coloration in animals in which surfaces that are exposed to light are dark colored and those that are shaded are light colored.

cyanobacteria   A moneran that contains chlorophyll as well as other accessory pigments and can carry out photosynthesis.

D

detritivore   An organism that feeds on dead and decaying matter.

detritus   Decaying organic matter that serves as a source of energy for detritivores.

DNA   Deoxyribonucleic acid; a molecule located in the nucleus of a cell that carries the genetic information that is responsible for running that cell.

dorsal   Situated on the back or upper side of an organism.

E

ecosystem   A group of organisms and the environment in which they live.

endoskeleton   An internal skeleton or support system such as the type found in vertebrates.

energy   The ability to do work.

epidermis   The outer, protective layer of cells on an organism, such as the skin.

exoskeleton   In crustaceans, a hard but flexible outer covering that supports and protects the body.

F

fish   A cold-blooded, aquatic vertebrate that has fins, gills, and scales and reproduces by laying eggs that are externally fertilized.

flagellum   A long, whiplike cellular extension that is used for locomotion or to create currents of water within the body of an organism.

food chain   The path that nutrients and energy follow as they are transferred through an ecosystem.

food web   Several interrelated food chains in an ecosystem.

fungus   An immobile heterotrophic organism that consumes its food by first secreting digesting enzymes on it, then absorbing the digested food molecules through the cell walls of threadlike hyphae.

G

gastrodermis   The layer of cells that lines the digestive cavity of a sponge or cnidarian, and the site at which nutrient molecules are absorbed.

gastropod   A class of arthropods that has either one shell or no shells, a distinct head equipped with sensory organs, and a muscular foot.

gill   A structure containing thin, highly folded tissues that are rich in blood vessels and serve as the sites where gases are exchanged in aquatic organisms.

glucose   A simple sugar that serves as the primary fuel in the cells of most organisms. Glucose is the product of photosynthesis.

H

herbivore   An animal that feeds on plants.

hermaphrodite   An animal in which both male and female sexual organs are present.

heterotroph   An organism that cannot make its own food and must consume plant or animal matter to meet its body's energy needs.

holdfast   The rootlike portion of a macroalga that holds the plant to the substrate.

hydrogen bond   A weak bond between the positive end of one polar molecule and the negative end of another.

hyphae   Filamentous strands that make up the bodies of fungi and form the threadlike extensions that produce digestive enzymes and absorb dissolved organic matter.

I

invertebrate   An animal that lacks a backbone, such as a sponge, cnidarian, worm, mollusk, or arthropod.

L

lateral   The region of the body that is along the side of an organism.

lateral line   A line along the side of a fish that connects to pressure-sensitive nerves that enable the fish to detect vibrations in the water.

larva   The newly hatched offspring of an animal that is structurally different from the adult form.

light   A form of electromagnetic radiation that includes infrared, visible, ultraviolet, and X-ray that travels in waves at the speed of 186,281 miles (300,000 km) per second.

M

mammal   A warm-blooded vertebrate that produces living young that are fed with milk from the mother's mammary glands.

mantle   A thin tissue that lies over the organs of a gastropod and secretes the shell.

mesoglea   A jellylike layer that separates the two cell layers in the bodies of sponges and cnidarians.

milt   A fluid produced by male fish that contains sperm and is deposited over eggs laid by the female.

mixotroph   An organism that can use the Sun's energy to make its own food or can consume food.

molt   Periodic shedding of an outer layer of shell, feathers, or hair that allows new growth to occur.

moneran   A simple, one-celled organism that neither contains a nucleus nor membrane-bound cell structures.

motile   Capable of moving from place to place.

N

nematocyst   In cnidarians, a stinging organelle that contains a long filament attached to a barbed tip that can be used in defense or to capture prey.

O

omnivore   An animal that eats both plants and animals.

operculum   In fish, the external covering that protects the gills. In invertebrates, a flap of tissue that can be used to close the opening in a shell, keeping the animal moist and protecting it from predators.

oviparous   An animal that produces eggs that develop and hatch outside the mother's body.

ovoviviparous   An animal that produces eggs that develop and hatch within the mother's body, then are extruded.

P

pectoral   An anatomical feature, such as a fin, that is located on the chest.

pelvic   An anatomical feature, such as a fin, that is located near the pelvis.

photosynthesis   The process in which green plants use the energy of sunlight to make nutrients.

plant   A nonmotile, multicellular organism that contains chlorophyll and is capable of making its own food.

polar molecule   A molecule that has a negatively charged end and a positively charged end.

polychaete   A member of a group of worms that has a segmented body and paired appendages.

posterior   The region near the tail or hind end of an organism.

productivity   The rate at which energy is used to convert carbon dioxide and other raw materials into glucose.

protist   A one-celled organism that contains a nucleus and membrane-bound cell structures such as ribosomes for converting food to energy and Golgi apparati for packaging cell products.

R

radula   A long muscle used for feeding that is covered with toothlike projections, found in most types of gastropods.

reptile   A cold-blooded, egg-laying terrestrial vertebrate whose body is covered with scales.

S

salinity   The amount of dissolved minerals in ocean water.

school   A group of aquatic animals swimming together for protection or to locate food.

sessile   Permanently attached to a substrate and therefore immobile.

setae   Hairlike bristles that are located on the segments of polychaete worms.

sexual reproduction   A type of reproduction in which egg and sperm combine to produce a zygote.

spawn   The act of producing gametes, or offspring, in large numbers, often in bodies of water.

spicule In sponges, a needle-like, calcified structure located in the body wall that provides support and protection.

spiracle An opening for breathing, such as the blowhole in a whale or the opening on the head of a shark or ray.

stipe A stemlike structure in a nonvascular plant.

surface tension A measure of how easy or difficult it is for molecules of a liquid to stick together due to the attractive forces between them.

swim bladder A gas-filled organ that helps a fish control its position in the water.

symbiosis A long-term association between two different kinds of organisms that usually benefits both in some way.

T

territorial behavior The defense of a certain area or territory by an animal for the purpose of protecting food, a mate, or offspring.

thallus The body of a macroalgae, made up of the blade, stipe, and holdfast.

V

ventral Situated on the stomach or lower side of an organism.

vertebrate A member of a group of animals with backbones, including fish, amphibian, reptiles, birds, and mammals.

viviparous An animal that gives birth to living offspring.

Z

zooxanthella A one-celled organism that lives in the tissues of invertebrates such as coral, sponge, or anemone where it carries out photosynthesis.

Further Reading and Web Sites

Books

Banister, Keith, and Andrew Campbell. *The Encyclopedia of Aquatic Life*. New York: Facts On File, 1985. Well written and beautifully illustrated book on all aspects of the ocean and the organisms in it.

Coulombe, Deborah A. *The Seaside Naturalist*. New York: Fireside, 1990. A delightful book for young students who are beginning their study of ocean life.

Davis, Richard A. *Oceanography: An Introduction to the Marine Environment*. Dubuque, Iowa: Wm. C. Brown Publishers, 1991. A text that helps students become familiar with and appreciate the world's oceans.

Dean, Cornelia. *Against the Tide*. New York: Columbia University Press, 1999. An analysis of the impact of humans and nature on the ever-changing beaches.

Ellis, Richard. *Encyclopedia of the Sea*. New York: Alfred A. Knopf, 2000. A factual, yet entertaining, compendium of sea life and lore.

Garrison, Tom. *Oceanography*. New York: Wadsworth Publishing, 1996. An interdisciplinary examination of the ocean for beginning marine science students.

Karleskint, George, Jr. *Introduction to Marine Biology*. Belmont, Calif.: Brooks/Cole-Thompson Learning, 1998. An enjoyable text on marine organisms and their relationships with one another and with their physical environments.

McCutcheon, Scott, and Bobbi McCutcheon. *The Facts On File Marine Science Handbook*. New York: Facts On File, 2003. An excellent resource that includes information on marine physical factors and living things as well as the people who have been important in ocean studies.

Nowak, Ronald M., et al. *Walker's Marine Mammals of the World*. Baltimore, Md.: Johns Hopkins University Press, 2003. An overview on the anatomy, taxonomy, and natural history of the marine mammals.

Pinet, Paul R. *Invitation to Oceanography*. Sudbury, Mass.: Jones and Bartlett Publishers, 2000. Includes explanations of the causes and effects of tides and currents, as well as the origins of ocean habitats.

Prager, Ellen J. *The Sea*. New York: McGraw-Hill, 2000. An evolutionary view of life in the Earth's oceans.

Reeves, Randall R., et al. *Guide to Marine Mammals of the World*. New York: Alfred A. Knopf, 2002. An encyclopedic work on sea mammals accompanied with gorgeous color plates.

Rice, Tony. *Deep Oceans*. Washington, D.C.: Smithsonian Museum Press, 2000. A visually stunning look at life in the deep ocean.

Sverdrup, Keith A., Alyn C. Duxbury, and Alison B. Duxbury. *An Introduction to the World's Oceans*. New York: McGraw Hill, 2003. A comprehensive text on all aspects of the physical ocean, including the seafloor and the ocean's physical properties.

Thomas, David. *Seaweeds*. Washington, D.C.: Smithsonian Museum Press, 2002. Illustrates and describes seaweeds from microscopic forms to giant kelps, explaining how they live, what they look like, and why humans value them.

Thorne-Miller, Boyce, and John G. Catena. *The Living Ocean*. Washington, D.C.: Friends of the Earth, 1991. A study of the loss of diversity in ocean habitats.

Waller, Geoffrey. *SeaLife: A Complete Guide to the Marine Environment*. Washington, D.C.: Smithsonian Institution Press, 1996. A text that describes the astonishing diversity of organisms in the sea.

Web Sites

Bird, Jonathon. *Adaptations for Survival in the Sea,* Oceanic Research Group, 1996. Available online. URL: http://www.oceanicresearch.org/adapspt.html. Accessed March 19, 2004. A summary and review of the educational film of the same name, which describes and illustrates some of the adaptations that animals have for life in salt water.

Buchheim, Jason. "A Quick Course in Ichthyology." Odyssey Expeditions. Available online. URL: http://www.marinebiology.org/fish.htm. Accessed January 4, 2004. A detailed explanation of fish physiology.

Duffy, J. Emmett. "Underwater urbanites: Sponge-dwelling napping shrimps are the only known marine animals to live in colonies that resemble the societies of bees and wasps." *Natural History*. December 2003. Available online. URL: http://www.findarticles.com/cf_dls/m1134/10_111736243/print.jhtml. Accessed January 2, 2004. A readable and fascinating explanation of eusocial behavior in shrimp and other animals.

"Fungus Farming in a Snail." *Proceedings of the National Academy of Science*, 100, no. 26 (December 4, 2003). Available online. URL: http://www.pnas.org/cgi/content/abstract/100/26/15643. A well-written, in-depth analysis of the ways that snails encourage the growth of fungi for their own food.

Gulf of Maine Research Institute Web site. Available online. URL: http://www.gma.org/about_GMA/default.asp. Accessed January 2, 2004. A comprehensive and up-to-date research site on all forms of marine life.

"Habitat Guides: Beaches and Shorelines." eNature. Available online. URL: http://www.enature.com/habitats/show_sublifezone.asp?sublifezoneID=60#Anchor-habitat-49575. Accessed November 21, 2003. A Web site with young people in mind that provides comprehensive information on habitats, organisms, and physical ocean factors.

Huber, Brian T. "Climate Change Records from the Oceans: Fossil Foraminifera." Smithsonian National Museum of Natural History. June 1993. Available online. URL: http://www.nmnh.si.edu/paleo/marine/foraminifera.htm. Accessed December 30, 2003. A concise look at the natural history of foraminifera.

King County's Marine Waters Web site. Available online. URL: http://splash.metrokc.gov/wlr/waterres/marine/index.htm. Accessed December 2, 2003. A terrific Web site on all aspects of the ocean, emphasizing the organisms that live there.

Mapes, Jennifer. "U.N. Scientists Warn of Catastrophic Climate Changes." National Geographic News. February 6, 2001. Available online. URL: http://news.nationalgeographic.com/news/2001/02/0206_climate1.html. A first-rate overview of the current data and consequences of global warming.

National Oceanic and Atmospheric Administration Web site. Available online. URL: http://www.noaa.gov/. A top-notch resource for news, research, diagrams, and photographs relating to the oceans, coasts, weather, climate, and research.

"Resource Guide, Elementary and Middle School Resources: Physical Parameters." Consortium for Oceanographic Activities for Students and Teachers. Available online. URL: http://www.coast-nopp.org/toc.html. Accessed December 10, 2003. A Web site for students and teachers that includes information and activities.

"Sea Snakes in Australian Waters." CRC Reef Research Centre. Available online. URL: http://www.reef.crc.org.au/discover/plantsanimals/seasnakes. Accessed November 18, 2004. An overview of sea snake classification, breeding, and venom.

"Index of Factsheets." Defenders of Wildlife. Available online. URL: http://www.kidsplanet.org/factsheets. Accessed November 18, 2004. Various species of marine animals are described on this excellent Web site suitable for both children and young adults.

U.S. Fish and Wildlife Service Web site. Available online. URL: http://www.fws.gov/. A federal conservation organization that covers a wide range of topics, including fisheries, endangered animals, the condition of the oceans, and conservation news.

"Conservation: Why Care About Reefs?" REN Reef Education Network, Environment Australia. Available online. URL: http//:www.reef.edu.au/asp_pages/search.asp. Accessed November 18, 2004. A superb Web site dedicated to the organisms living in and the health of the coral reefs.

Index